Introducing the Bible

Jaime & Will Riddle

4th Edition

Table of Contents

Introduction

The library of books about the Bible is amazingly vast. There are commentaries, dictionaries, textbooks, and references all designed to help you get scholarly meaning out of the Word. But a basic overview of the text is often all that is necessary to start getting more out of the text. This book hopes to help fill that gap.

We cover three main topic areas which are not usually combined. First are issues about approaching the Bible. What is the Bible? Can we trust it? How did we get it? This section of the book brings together an array of information that will increase your confidence about the Bible and help you get started with it.

The second section offers an overview of the Bible's contents from a very high level. What are the important stories? How is it arranged? What are the themes of the Old and New Testaments? How are they similar but different? This kind of orientation helps you understand the story and themes of the text. It also helps you bridge the Biblical past with the present day and future to come.

Then we end with a rather academic section on how to get meaning out of the Biblical text. Our conviction is that the trends of the last century have not placed enough emphasis on how to make the Bible personally valuable. How do we get meaning that breathes life into our spirit and changes us?

It is our hope that presenting these pieces of how to read the Bible will help you understand it better and walk with Jesus more closely.

~ Part I ~
Approaching the Bible

Chapter 1:
What is the Bible?

Whether you were born in church, or are new to seeking God, you might have heard quite a bit about the Bible... but what is it?

The Bible is not just a religious book. It is your invitation to meet the living God. It is God's personal message to you. Everything in its pages tell you what you need to know in order to come into a relationship with Him, both now and for eternity.

A LOVING GOD

The fact that we have a Bible at all means that God is a loving, revealing God. He wants you to know who He is. He wants you to know what He is like, and not like. He wants you to know that you can be in His presence always, and how to do that.

This means God is loving. He cares. Only a loving and redemptive God would present this opportunity.

A RESCUE OPERATION

If the Bible is an invitation to come into relationship with the living God, then implicit in this invitation is the understanding that you are naturally not in relationship with God. You need rescuing.

Without God reaching out to rescue you, you would not know Him. You might have a sense of His presence or existence at times, but you would not know much more than that. You would have lots of questions and few answers. The Bible calls this situation, being "lost." You would feel lost, like a child abandoned by its father.

But God has not abandoned you. He is a good Father who cares about each one of His children. He could have left people alone in the darkness, but because of His great love, He has made a pathway back to Himself.

The Bible was written to show you this pathway. You may know things aren't quite right in your world, but don't know why. You may have a sense the world is flawed, that others are flawed, and life is flawed. Perhaps you realize you are flawed! That is because you need God and so does everyone else.

God wants you to come into relationship with Him and surrender your relationship to a lost and dying world. The Bible shows you this way of escape and invites you into a new way.

A Message of Reconciliation

A main theme in the Bible is that God's diagnosis for all of the world's problems is *reconciliation*, or reuniting mankind to Himself. It isn't better systems, more money, or more knowledge. God first wants to restore the broken fellowship between each individual and Himself.

He knows if He does this, then everything else will get better afterwards. The life and love of God will fill each person, and then pour out to others. Scripture calls this "abiding in the vine." If we each tap into the love of God, individually, the life-giving flow will fix many things.

Scripture also tells us that there is only way to tap into this life-giving flow, and that is through Jesus Christ. There are a thousand ways humanity seeks spirituality, and a thousand things people call "God." But the Bible says there is only one path to the true and living God. It is through the Savior of the World, Jesus Christ, who died on the Cross to reconcile us to God.

This is not just a story contained in the Bible. The entire Bible points us to Jesus. It leads us through what He did, how that worked, and why we should believe in Him. It explains how Jesus' death reconciled us to the Father by *redeeming* us, or purchasing

10

us back. The Bible's message is that you cannot redeem yourself because you have been taken captive by sin. Sin keeps people enslaved to worlds of their own making where they are discouraged from seeking God or His ways. Jesus came to invade these worlds and bring us all back to the source of life.

In a way, both Jesus' coming and the Bible are forms of divine interruption. They show how God reaches into our world even though people hate Him or don't think they need Him. The key to reading the Bible is therefore reading it through the lens of love: God seeking reconciliation with His people.

The next few chapters will go into great detail about the Bible's characters, plot, and themes, but in the end, the main message is that God loves His children and wants as many of them as possible to walk with Him, both now and in eternity.

A REDEMPTIVE HISTORY

Knowing the Bible is an invitation to walking with God is great—that's the big picture—but now what do we do about what's actually in it? Many people get hung up as soon as they start reading their Bible because it is like being transported back to an ancient world that doesn't make much sense. It's easy to get put off by the vocabulary and trying to figure out what's going on.

The best way to approach the contents of the Bible is to realize it is a history of God redeeming mankind, a *redemptive history.* It is a chronicle of God working with man to counter and displace evil, by creating a godly Kingdom that will witness love, truth, and life to the ends of the earth.

The redemptive history of the Bible starts in the book of Genesis. In the very beginning, God creates man in His image and walks with him. God commissions the first couple, Adam and Eve, to create this godly Kingdom. But they are deceived in their first encounter with evil. They disobey, quickly causing humanity to get off the right path and lose God.

Mankind plunges into the depths of sin and death, and God successively outreaches to man, trying to restore him to the heights from which he has fallen. For the most part, however, humanity doesn't want God anymore. So, God works with people in steps, like rungs on a ladder, to get us back. Each book of the Bible adds a little more of the story behind working up these steps.

Now some people struggle with seeing the Bible in a positive light—especially the Old Testament—because large portions of it are about war and negative things. To be sure, parts of the Bible are hard to read through. This is because it is a real history, not a fairy tale. Redemption occurs eventually, but it's very rocky along the way.

The Old Testament describes the Father's redemptive mission beginning with one people group—Israel, whose name in Hebrew means "shall struggle/rule/prevail with God." Much of the Old Testament shows God intervening to build relationships with people while they run and resist at every turn—thus the war and negative things.

Yet the New Testament describes how this redemptive mission ends, with God and His people indeed prevailing and gaining the upper hand. Through Jesus, people all over the globe have chosen from their hearts to follow God and do the right thing.

In other words, the quest to conquer sin, death, and deception is a struggle for God and man together... but in the end, they win! The source of evil is dethroned and promised to be destroyed, with those believing in Christ escaping that destruction and being restored to God eternally. This means that the Bible can and should be read through the lens of hope—even the negative-sounding portions. Redemption triumphs!

WHY THE BIBLE?

In circles outside the Church, it is popular to hold the Bible in disrepute. Many would like to get rid of its influence on society and people's beliefs. This begs the question, what would the world be like without the Bible?

Sadly, history has actually shown us what it would be like. For more than two thousand years before Christ, the world at large (except for the Jews) had no Bible. Without God's special truths and principles, the condition of world was described in Romans 1. Men were darkened in their understanding and had unnatural relationships with each other. They worshipped idols, animals, and the creation instead of the Creator. Without the Bible, the ancient world was dark. It was filled with religious distortion, with gods, demigods, shamans, and tokens.

Interestingly though, ancient societies knew that God (or gods) existed without the Bible. Ancient man instinctively knew there was a divine being from looking at nature, himself, and his fellow man. Most societies also believed in an afterlife, sacrifices, spirits, and demonic forces. The book of Romans explains how the concept of God was embedded in creation, and that the Gentiles not having the Law were sometimes obedient to it (2:14). Many ancient societies believed, for example. that stealing and murdering were wrong. Some made law codes that echoed parts of the Ten Commandments. They didn't need a Bible to tell them to do so.

On the other hand, because the absolute Law of God wasn't known, tribes and civilizations varied in the morals they emphasized. Some punished murder within their tribe, but accepted murdering someone from another tribe, for example. Many civilizations employed mass human sacrifice, even while trying to protect its own people from death.

Cultures unreached by the Bible today still vary in their understanding of "general" or *natural law*. There is a sense of conscience and obeying the rules of society, but what is good and evil differs widely. So is what people consider helpful, healthy, proper, and profane.

The same was true for ancient man's knowledge of God. No-one needed a Bible to know there was an invisible God in heaven. Many ancient cultures worshipped a sky-god or creator-god in the heavens. Most also had a creation myth, a Fall myth, and a Flood (or destruction of the world) myth. Mankind knew there was something special about him but wasn't sure what. He knew he was separated from God but wasn't sure why. Nor was he sure how to reach back up to God and get in His good graces again.

This is why most ancient religions worshipped their gods with sacrifices and rituals. If you research the common religions of indigenous America, Africa, Asia, or Europe, you find they all had priests, prayers, and temples. But their gods were deaf and blind and could not answer their prayers for protection or blessing. Most ancient peoples were afraid their gods would turn on them at any moment and smite their village, crops, or empire. Most had terrible practices they had to obey because they believed their gods demanded them—human sacrifice, child sacrifice, cult prostitutes, and things which were abhorrent to the real God, as Romans 1 explains.

Missionaries still see these things every day, but modern man is relatively unaware of them because atheism has deeply penetrated our society. Although atheism seems so normal today, did you know it is actually a modern invention? You have to be taught not to believe. In fact, civilizations in all times and all continents have been religious until relatively recently.

So the God of the Bible brought into the world, a written revelation of His will. In writing, God was able to progressively and permanently reveal his true nature to the world.

HOW THE BIBLE CAME TO BE

God's first written revelation came through Moses, in approximately 1500BC. In the middle of ancient Egypt, where the pyramids and mummies signified the beliefs of their society, Moses spoke the prophetic words, "Let My people go!" Speaking from the very heart of God, he delivered the Hebrew people out of darkness physically and then spiritually. Through Genesis, Exodus, Leviticus, Numbers, and Deuteronomy, Moses gave them a written law code with an inspired history of Creation and their origins.

God spoke truth and principles to them, to reform them from their pagan ways. He addressed the children of Abraham who were worshipping a golden calf with why they shouldn't do so, and what they should do instead.

Over time, more pieces of truth came into the picture and the Bible grew. It began to encompass wisdom and prophecy, history, and psalms. The amount of truth Israel had kept growing, but being in a living relationship with God was difficult for many of them. Often, they turned to pagan gods with the benefits and pleasures associated with them.

Meanwhile, the non-believing world grew in its futility. Thinkers and philosophers started writing down what they thought spiritual truth was. The ancient world gave birth to Hinduism, Buddhism, Confucianism, Platonism, and all sorts of alternative religions. These enslaved societies under them, capturing them into systems where they worshipped cattle, the earth, ancestors, or emptiness.

After several thousand years of human history, the world finally got access to the full truth! The full nature of God was revealed when the New Testament was penned and closed, around 90AD. After Jesus came, it became clear what all the sacrifices meant, what priests and temples foreshadowed, and what God really wanted from man. God's true nature became known, and with it, special revelations such as heaven and hell, angels, salvation, and the Trinity.

Over the next thousand years, scholars in the Dark Ages and Middle Ages specialized in discovering and codifying these revelations in Scripture. Then in the Protestant era, around 1500AD, the full Bible began to be printed in different languages. People all over Europe began to reform their societies based on systematic study of the Word. Massive changes began as the Bible began to be applied to common, everyday matters.

Building civilization on these truths is what launched the world into the modern era. In Europe, nation after nation began reforming its political, economic, social, and religious systems based on principles in Scripture. Laws changed, humanitarianism changed, science developed, diplomacy began. Then came America, started by a radical group of Christians committed to trying to build a nation the way God intended it, from the beginning.

The world we know today could not have come into existence without the special revelations in God's Word. This is what made Western civilization so different from any other in history. It is easy to think that progress just occurred, either at some magic point, or just gradually over time. But it was neither magic nor time that made things the way they are—it was God's truths written down in the Bible, working their way through all the spheres of society.

How do we really know that the Bible did this? For thousands of years before Scripture was widely available, humanity stayed basically the same. There were some advanced civilizations, some law codes, some engineering and wealth from the beginning. But it was far from universal and often under the thumb of some tyrant. For most of history, there was no such thing as human rights, individual rights, or equal opportunity. Unfortunately, most people suffered and died nameless, faceless, and young. Many also died in spiritual bondage or deception.

It wasn't until the Bible came along and elevated mankind out of darkness by reasserting the true God, the true history of what had happened to man, and the true way to come back into fellowship, that the world became anything like the place it is today. You can see this when you go to an unreached culture today. "Unreached" by what? The life-giving principles the Bible teaches, and the life-giving systems it can create.

So the purpose of the Bible is not to know that there is a God. Nor is it to discover that humanity is special, creation is special, and there's something divine but flawed about the world—many cultures without the Bible know these things. But the Bible tells us the secrets behind why things are the way they are, and what the unique solution is. God gives us this privileged information because He loves us and wants to provide the terms by which we can make it back to Him.

WHAT THE BIBLE CLAIMS TO BE

As Christians, we believe that the Bible is God's Word, which means His truth revealed to us in written form. We also believe it is divinely inspired by His spirit, the Holy Spirit.

Some have said that this was an idea made up by Jews or Christians during the course of history, to give themselves moral authority. But this is not an idea made up by men, it is what the Bible teaches about itself. It claims,

> *All Scripture is **God-breathed** and useful for instruction, for conviction, for correction, and for training in righteousness, so that the man of God may be complete, fully equipped for every good work.... (2 Timothy 3:16-17)*

In many ways, the Bible puts itself on the record as the holy, divine, inspired Word of God. In the Old Testament, Moses records that he met with God face to face on Mount Sinai and received revelation straight from Him. For forty days, Moses was instructed so much that his face glowed when he came down off the mountain. People were so afraid, he had to hide his face with a veil.

Then Moses unveiled what God had told him when he wrote down the first five books of the Bible. These revealed the inspired history and law code God wanted His people to live by. Scripture says the Ten Commandments were actually written by the finger of God Himself (Exodus 31:18, Deut. 9:10)!

Later came the prophets who also spoke the Word of God. About them, Scripture says,

> "No prophecy ever had origin in the human will, but prophets, though men, **spoke from God** as they were carried along by the Holy Spirit" (2 Peter 1:21).

Accordingly, the prophets claimed divine inspiration by prefacing their words with, "Thus sayeth the Lord," or "The Lord spoke to me saying..." These were not said lightly. Sometimes the Lord did incredible things to prepare His prophets to receive His divine words such as burning Isaiah's mouth with a coal or making Ezekiel radically fast.

Sometimes miracles following a prophecy testified that what the prophets were saying was from God, such as when Elisha commanded Naaman to bathe in the river to cure his leprosy (2 Kings 5). Even unbelievers discovered that God was behind His prophets' words when, for example, Elijah called fire down in front of the Baal worshippers (1 Kings 18).

Similarly, words of knowledge from the prophets often convinced people they were hearing from God, such as when Joseph and Daniel interpreted their emperor's dreams and predicted the seasons to come. The Lord's prophets knew they were speaking the direct words of God and wrote them down on scrolls for future generations to know the ways of God. Eventually these formed "the Law and the Prophets" which Israel built their society on, up until the time of Jesus.

Jesus also claimed Scripture was the divine Word of God—not just His followers in later centuries. He quoted Scripture to defeat Satan during His temptation in the wilderness. This alone should testify to the inspiration and authority of the Word. But just to drill the point home to man and Satan, Jesus also added that man did not live on bread alone but on "every *word* that proceeds *out of the mouth of God*" (Matthew 4:4).

Jesus also said it was not His own words He taught, but those of the Father (John 14:24). He quoted Scripture, taught it, and obeyed it. Not only did He abide by the principles of the Law, but He fulfilled all its requirements so we could be free. His entire life, including His sacrifice, was a validation of Scriptural truth.

This includes the Old Testament. It's important to bring up this point because many Christians believe the Old Testament deserves second-rate status compared to the New Testament. It is true that Jesus revised the spirit of the Law and did away with its ceremonial practices—because He was the King who obeyed it and the High Priest who made perfect atonement.

Yet Jesus upheld the Old Testament's authority with His words and actions. He did not contradict the Law or invalidate it. He said about the Old Testament, if unbelievers could not listen to Moses, how would they listen to Him? (John 5:47). Paul clarified that the Old Testament laws and prophets were supposed to be a "tutor" to Jesus (Gal. 3:24)—and a tutor is a teacher that goes away when its student internalizes what is being taught.

Also remember that in New Testament times, the only "Scripture" available was the Old Testament. So when Jesus taught the Word of God in the Temple and taught the disciples on the road to Emmaus everything concerning Him that was "in all the Scriptures," those were Old Testament Scriptures (Luke 24:26). When the Ethiopian eunuch was enlightened and moved by the Scriptures, he was reading the book of Isaiah. We note that 2 Timothy 3:16 said, "All Scripture is God-breathed..."

This means that the Old Testament is just as divine as the New. We must revise it in the light of the Cross, which all things in the Old Testament point to, but God does not have another standard for holiness or absolute morality. Jesus fulfills those standards for us but does not abolish them:

> *Do not think that I have come to abolish the Law or the Prophets. I have not come to abolish them, but to fulfill them. For I tell you truly,*

until heaven and earth pass away, not a single jot, not a stroke of a pen, will disappear from the Law until everything is accomplished. So then, whoever breaks one of the least of these commandments and teaches others to do likewise will be called least in the kingdom of heaven; but whoever practices and teaches them will be called great in the kingdom of heaven. (Matt. 5:17-19)

This means we can't say, as some do today for example, that Jesus did away with the concept of sin because He said we should love each other. This is forming your own religion out of a few verses you like while ignoring Jesus' own view of Scripture.

DIVINE INSPIRATION

The Bible claims the Old and New Testaments are the divine Word of God, spoken by Him out of His mouth. Not all "holy" texts claim to be this. Secular people often scoff that all religions are the same, but not only are they not the same, their sacred texts are not.

The Hindu Vedas, for example, make no claim of self-divinity. Neither do the writings of Buddha, who himself insisted he was not divine. The Bible has a unique theology about it being "the Living Word," or the "Word made flesh" (John 1:14). This equates the text with the person of Jesus—both sustain man and lead to eternal life. It is the highest claim of authority that any religious text has ever made about itself.

Of course the Bible itself, the literal pages, are not divine—it is the message within it. This is important because other sacred books, like the Quran, are considered to be divine and holy because of their paper and ink. But Jesus said the Scriptures bear witness of Him, and only in that way are they divine—they lead to divine life (John 5:39). It's an important distinction.

So how did God's bring His Word to us? The Bible teaches a very unique method of inspiration, which upholds its claim of being divine and distinguishes it from other holy books.

We go back to 2 Timothy 3:16 again, which says the Word of God is "God-breathed." The word "God-breathed" is sometimes translated "inspired by God." It comes from the idea of breathing life into something, which is what God did to Adam, and what Jesus did to His disciples (John 20:22). Both imply the breath of eternal life, the Holy Spirit, which gives life to our mortal bodies (Romans 8:11).

Similarly, God breathed the words of the Scripture to give you new life—not just physically, but spiritually. Reading it is supposed to continually bring you back to Jesus, where eternal life is found.

The way you receive revelation from the Scriptures is similar to the way God inspired men to write it. He breathed life into the authors of Scripture, activating them to write it—the same way He breathes life into you and activates you to understand or behave. This method of inspiration is very real and relatable. It reflects God's character and the kind of relationship He wants to have with His people. When God inspired His authors, He allowed them to keep their personalities and identities intact. He didn't overshadow them in a mystical trance and dictate the words of Scripture through them like a loudspeaker. Instead, he allowed them to express themselves uniquely.

This is why each Biblical author has his own literary style, ways they looked at things, and arguments and analogies they use. In the four gospels there are linguistic and stylistic differences, even while explaining the same event. God allowed His message to flow through many kinds of people without sacrificing their humanness.

In contrast, the Book of Mormon is said to have been given to Joseph Smith from the angel of Moroni while Smith was in a trance. Smith himself was not actively engaged in the task of writing but wrote passively while a mystical force took him and the dictation over. Additionally, this divine discharge was accomplished very quickly; Smith wrote his text, with a few scribes, in just 65 days. The Bible was written by about 40 different authors over a period of 1500 years.

The same method of inspiration is attributed to the Qur'an, which was dictated to Mohammed from the angel Gabriel. Mohammed was, like Smith, alone and wrote his text that was mystically dictated by some kind of spiritual force.

And a similar style is ascribed to the Buddha as he was overshadowed in mystical meditation, sometimes after extreme hours of prayer and fasting where he almost starved to death.

Now Biblical prophets sometimes had dreams and visions, and they sometimes fasted, but they transcribed their messages under very normal circumstances. Jeremiah 36, for example, details how Jeremiah's scribe wrote down several years of Jeremiah's prophecies as Jeremiah spoke them to him in the daytime, under normal conditions. But then the scroll that the scribe wrote on was burned, so he had to do it again! Jeremiah's prophecies were not so sacred or mystical that the same revelation from God could not pour forth again in a repeat scenario.

Another time, Ezekiel was required to radically fast and pray for visions concerning Israel, but God gave him specific instructions about how he was to eat and sleep throughout. His health and wits were therefore intact. God did not have his divine authors contort their bodies, souls, or spirits in any kind of way. No substances or duress were involved, nor mystical translations from angels, etc.

On the other extreme, the Bible does not support the idea of God simply allowing the most gifted or holy individuals to write Scripture all on their own—as if they didn't need God at all. For example, God didn't let Moses and Daniel, who were exceptionally well-educated, write down a history one day and share it with everybody as God's inspired account.

This view of inspiration fits closely with the Hindu Vedas, however. The Vedas do not claim to be divine but rather a collected work of scriptures written by some of Hinduism's most enlightened men. Hindu scholars do not agree on the authority of the writers, the age or origin of them, or which approach to Hinduism is the most enlightened since there are conflicting views of how it should be practiced.

Notably the Vedas have the opposite problem of the Book of Mormon and the Qur'an—the number of authors and scriptures are so voluminous that very few Hindu teachers have ever read all of them. The average Hindu has access to only partial bits of their sacred literature. These are taught through a variety of methods, and not printed as a holy book that each common person can have.

If the Bible were more like the Vedas, it too would likely be a lot larger and scattered of a work as well, considering the number of great scholars and teachers within the Judeo-Christian tradition. Fortunately, God managed to condense His message into a moderate size, and transmit it through a few dozen men with very public ministries to verify their veracity.

And although the Biblical authors lived in very different time periods and different regions, the same basic message trumpets forth—that God is working to redeem mankind through atonement and create a Kingdom where He can dwell among them. Each book of the Bible develops the same themes, and the story builds upon itself as the centuries pass during its writing. The only way this could have happened is if God inspired these men to write, and His Spirit really was with them, speaking the same things.

This **middle view** of inspiration which says the entire text of the Bible, including the individual words, is a product of the mind of God expressed in human terms or conditions, is called **plenary inspiration**. Peter puts it more simply:

> *"Above all, you must understand that no prophecy of Scripture came about by the prophet's own interpretation. For prophecy never had its origin in the will of man, but men spoke from God as they were carried along by the Holy Spirit." (2 Peter 1:20-21).*

The idea of being "carried along" by the Holy Spirit is a key concept. Because we don't believe God took over and dictated the Scripture for the Biblical authors, we don't have to get worked up over minor errors like whether 1 Kings 10:26 said 140 or 1400 chariots. It's not that details don't matter. It's just that some parts of the parts of the Bible are more than 3000 years old, and a great deal of manual copying was required to bring them through to us. We recognize that while the original words of God were perfect, and the original manuscripts probably were, there are only copies now, and copies of copies. Small transition errors occurred through the ages, and more can be expected to turn up as archaeology continues.

But it is only when you get into the wrong spirit that you feel like the Bible might not be *inerrant* (without error) if every little letter and number isn't perfect! There has been lots of quibbling over these kinds of things in the past, and among Christians, which really only encourages skeptics' claims that the Bible is unreliable.

In reality, there is no content in the Bible that is really under question. To this date, no transmission error has ever been substantiated that would impact a major teaching, person, or event of the Bible. God has protected His Word.

But is the idea of just one divine book from God even reasonable? Don't people live and die for what they think are divine books all the time? Well, not exactly. Jews and Christians are the main believers with a tradition of dying for their Scripture. We have such faith in our Word partly because we know that during the time Scripture was written, prophets were killed if they falsely testified of the Lord. They were publicly executed if they lied or prophesied falsely—which people could tell, if their predictions didn't come true.

And, ironically, the Bible itself is the source of such strict punishments. Moses wrote them as part of God's protective protocol. Imagine if Mohammed had told people that they could kill him on the spot, or anyone who spoke for him, if he was found to be lying. This is what Moses' Law commanded the Jews to do for centuries, as prophets spoke to kings and put their words "on the record."

This gives a huge amount of credibility to Scriptural authors and the Prophets because the stakes were so high if they were found to be wrong. God made the standard so high so that first Israel, and then the Church, could build on what He was speaking.

For its part, the New Testament didn't dilute the standard much. Jesus got in trouble with the Pharisees—and was ultimately executed—for ostensibly revising the words of Moses and the Prophets. But they thought they were simply following Moses' rule! Their zeal to execute Jesus based on the difference between His interpretations and their own shows the kind of vigilance that protected the Scriptures for centuries.

The rest of the New Testament is similarly firm on protecting the integrity of the Word. Jesus says that those who lead the young astray would be better off if they had millstones tied around their necks and were drowned in the sea. Paul says that anyone who preaches any other gospel is to be accursed (Gal. 1:6-8) or sent to hell. He confronts multiple false doctrines and their teachers who were leading others astray—at one point even saying they should castrate themselves (Gal. 5:12)! The Book of Revelation adds that condemnation to hell is deserved for those who add or take away words from its prophecy (22:18-19).

These warnings to New Testament prophets and teachers certainly add confidence to the claim that Scripture is God-breathed. There are, and always have been, the very highest punishments at stake for corrupting the message.

GOD'S WORD HAS POWER

Many in our culture have given people the impression that the Bible is very heavy—that God is putting burdens on people that are too hard to bear. Nothing could be further from the truth. God is looking to lift burdens.

God's Word is living and active, which means it has the power to change you. It's unlike any other book ever written, and its power isn't mystical. It's a fact of the Holy Spirit searching your heart as you read, to expose your true thoughts. As the writer of Hebrews says,

> "For the word of God is living and active, sharper than any double-edged sword, it penetrates even to dividing soul and spirit, joints and marrow; it judges the thoughts and attitudes of the heart." (Hebrews 4:11-12)

This means God won't let you keep your inner hurts and motives hidden. The normal thing is to cover them up and try to present your good side to God. But God doesn't want your works or your goodness. He wants humility and brokenness. So he illumines the dark places in our hearts as we read, and shows us in plain view what is broken so we can come to Him and get it fixed.

In this way, God likens the Bible to a hammer, a sword, and a fire. All of these things are tools which prevent you from staying as you are.

When you bring God's truth to bear in the larger world around you, it will not just change you, it will change others. It will change everyone who obeys it, even a whole society. This is what happened in the old Roman Empire. Jesus came and started a cultural revolution with twelve disciples. They reached out to others, planted churches, and preached the Bible. Slowly, the Roman Empire which persecuted them became less hostile to Christianity. And eventually, it adopted it as their official religion.

This process took 300 years, but the more it was accepted, the more it could change. Around 400AD, Christianity turned the heart of the Roman Empire against the barbaric gladiatorial games. A Christian monk named Telemachus jumped into the ring crying out for this horrid practice to stop, upon which he was immediately stoned by the crowd. The emperor, however, was so impressed by the martyrdom that he immediately worked to end throwing slaves, Christians, and undesirables to the beasts.

Christianity civilized many other aspects of Greco-Roman culture, and of warrior cultures outside its borders. As more and more people corporately came into a relationship with Jesus, and read the Bible, what seemed normal or pleasurable to them started changing.

This can be seen in the modern age, for example in India. For thousands of years, Hinduism has mired India in idolatry, polytheism, and temple worship. People have shrines in their homes and conduct daily rituals to commune with the gods, but are held in bondage by doctrines of passivity and permanence. Their sacred texts teach that your current station in life reflects how good you were in your last life, and if you're in a bad place, it is because your spirit is poor.

For most of their history, this fixed Indian society in a caste system, where today over 200 million people at the bottom are still seen as less worthy than animals. They are forced to shovel dung, dispose of the dead, or work on slave labor sites. Millions more suffer from poverty and disease because of sacred beliefs regarding cattle; their cattle must be washed in the rivers they use and never killed, even in times of famine. India's environment, economy, and well-being of people have suffered, yet nothing in the Hindu worldview discourages this. In fact, the Vedas teach it is futile to try to change anything; it is against the will of the gods.

As Indians have pursued contemporary Western values, however, including Christianity, the Bible has begun to confront some of their longest-held values. The Vedas portray the world as an animistic, random place, so there is no rationale for science or progress. But the Bible portrays the world as an objective, ordered system, which supports research and engineering. The Vedas' worldview is that life is uncreated and infinite, with mystical reasons why you are where you are. But the worldview of the Bible says that life is short, created by a personal God who wants you to change your destiny and bless others. As more people have acted on these kinds of beliefs, Indian society has changed and prospered.

Cultural shifts like these, along with the millions of individuals who are causing them, are evidence that the Bible is an encounter with the living God. It's not just a cliché. The Bible is a catalyst for change, from the living heart behind it.

This makes the Bible unique among other religious texts. Not because it affects culture—that is true for any religion—but because it gently brings peace and justice. The Bible helped create the modern conscience which is sensitive to the poor and suffering, and desirous of systems that will change it. Things weren't always that way. The Bible created the desire to extend progress, human rights, property rights, and prosperity across the world. It created sensitivity to children, animals, and the environment. It formed the foundation of our reasoning about fairness and tolerance.

When people stand up for these sorts of values, whether they are Christian or not, they are standing up for the world the Bible helped create.

You can see this when you go to other areas of the world which have not been discipled by the Bible. They are very different from us. It's hard to negotiate an Arab-Israeli peace, for example, because Islamic values are so different from Christianity's. Islam doesn't teach peace; it values holy war. Its sacred text, the Qur'an, orders the annihilation of Israel and the conquest of the rest of the world. The stated goal is to get rid of the other faiths through whatever means necessary to purify the world for Allah. Conquest can be by the sword, colonialism, slavery, or any method since the Qur'an teaches that what matters to Allah is submission, not heart conversion.

Simply put, what a civilization values, comes from its religion. And whether it has power to achieve it, comes from its sacred text. Importantly, the Bible doesn't just tell you what to value or change. It takes you to the source of change, Jesus Christ. It causes person after person to encounter truths about the world and themselves which, if you submit to them, will change you. The transforming power of divine truth lodged in your spirit will start to affect the world around you. You become fundamentally different. You become a vessel He can flow through.

As more and more people accept what Jesus does, they start a new life and He gives them the power to change to be like Him too. As this happens on a large scale, entire cultures change into His image. Whatever was lost and unfilled by God in the past starts getting addressed until society becomes more reflective of the hope in God. The more cultural hostility to Christianity drops, the more changes can be made which reflect Biblical principles. A society becomes more like God—more peaceful, loving, and free.

This is what we mean when we say the Word comes with power and authority. It has the ability to transform all things that submit to what it has to say. First you, by giving you access to heavenly wisdom and power. Then believers corporately, who unite to bring more of God's will from heaven to earth.

THE IMPLICATION OF INSPIRATION

In the Bible, God has given the world a personal package of eternal truths, collectively preserved over thousands of years. He has hand-picked the information we need to know in order to believe His Word and come into relationship with Him. It is like a love letter. God has reached down through time and space to write to us, to connect to us through His own words.

To personalize this, imagine a lover who spent their whole life reaching out to you. Then imagine that even though you were angry and depraved, they promised you love, life, and happiness forever. Imagine they were willing to be with you, share all their riches with you, and tell you all their important secrets. Then suddenly, they sacrificed their life for you—died for you—and left you a note telling you all about their ultimate concern for your welfare.

Except... what if they didn't just write one note? What if they sent their message of love and devotion through dozens of others, to transmit it to you? Imagine that some of them wrote you cards, while others sent you emails, texts, made a YouTube video, or used whatever medium they felt most comfortable expressing themselves through.

This is God. He inspired dozens of people to write to you, over time, in different kinds of ways with variations on the same theme. Then they transmitted this message to you in the best way they could— through poetry and wisdom, history and prophecy, etc.

Keep this in mind as you read through the Bible and come across the tangents and bunny trails, different formats and emphases— they are all just part of His great love letter. Each story weaves back into His eternal purpose of doing for you, what you could not do for Him. So many people died in this story, to show His love. Some died living it, while others died writing it. Some even died just to be able to print this story in your own language for you. Will you believe it?

Chapter 2:
Is the Bible Reliable?

The Christian faith rests upon the premise that the Old and New Testaments are real—that the people, events, and ideas in them really are true. But talking to people who are hostile to the Bible can cause doubt. It's easy to feel as if it is just your belief against their disbelief, or your word against theirs. The question comes down to: If you believe the Bible is true, and someone else doesn't, who is to say which person is wrong? Isn't it just a matter of opinion?

Actually, it isn't! When you study the authenticity of the Bible, you find that the scales are significantly tipped in your favor. It is more likely than not that the Bible is true. It is more reasonable to believe in it, than not to believe in it. Studies show that the Bible is an extremely reliable document—even *the most reliable document of the entire ancient world.*

RELIABILITY TESTS

Really? Most people have never heard this before. How can that be?

When confirming how reliable an ancient document is, experts look to different things. First, they look at **_internal evidence_**—what the document claims about itself, and whether it is consistent. For the Bible, this means experts look at whether the prophets' predictions came true, and whether they validate each other. They look to see if the Bible confirms what it says in its own pages, or if there is contradictory evidence—for example, if in one place it claims to be God's Word, but in another place says it is not.

Then they look at ***external evidence***—whether the Bible is validated by things in history, geography, or the known world of that time. Archaeologists, for example, examine whether excavation and artifacts confirm places and events in the Bible. Historians look to see if people and dates can be confirmed in historical records. Many scholars have spent much time studying fine details in the Bible to see if its descriptions of marriage, trade, languages, and war customs fit the historical understanding of those times.

Other scholars see if what has been said in the past makes sense with what we observe today. Anthropologists, for example, may compare what Jews currently believe to Biblical history, to see if the Bible's claims extend to fit reality. They also look at hostile sources of information, such as narratives from Egypt, Assyria, Babylon, and Canaanite civilization. Islamic tradition actually corroborates many early Genesis events, for example, Cush and Mizriam's entrance to Egypt, and Ishmael and Isaac's tense relationship. These all provide external validity to Biblical history.

In the area of external evidence, the rule is: the more hostile the scholar or the source material, the more evidence there is for Biblical integrity if the study confirms the text. It should be noted that the majority of scholars examining the Bible in the last two centuries have been skeptical of its claims, not sympathetic. However, this is what makes the findings that the Bible is so reliable, so rock solid. Some skeptics have even converted during their studies because of the evidence.

Lastly, examiners may do a ***comparison test***, which looks at how one ancient document's reliability compares to other ancient documents. This often comes down to researching how many copies of manuscripts exist, how old they are, and how accurate they are in comparison to one another.

Almost unbelievably, the Bible passes all these tests to the highest degree. In fact, to date, no meaningful bit of evidence has yet overturned anything the Bible says. It has stood up to the most hostile witnesses against it, as well as the test of time.

COMPARISON TO OTHER ANCIENT WORKS

Unbelievers are skeptical of relying on a book which is very old, and that's a valid concern. But just as God provided a second set of tablets to Moses after he dropped the first set, God has protected His entire Word, the Bible, throughout its lifetime. Mankind has not been able to destroy it or blot it out. God has preserved it through natural and supernatural ways.

Still, can you really trust a document that started being written over 3500 years ago? Compared to other ancient texts people believe in today, the answer is a definite "yes."

Number of Manuscripts. In comparison to other ancient documents, the Bible is the most historically reliable document of the ancient world. It is hard to overestimate this finding.

Today, secular information on ancient Egypt, Greece, and Rome is considered very reliable. Entire college programs revolve around ancient secular sources without anyone worrying they might be fallible. You yourself might have been taught information about ancient Greeks and Romans as though it were "gospel"—as completely solid and believable. Yet the sources which verify those ancient civilizations are not nearly as old and reliable as the sources that verify the Bible!

First, the New Testament has over 24,600 ancient copies. This makes it the most well-attested book in history. The second most common ancient book is Homer's Iliad, which has 643 ancient copies. When you research the reliability of ancient documents, you will find that most professional articles and organizations reference the Bible because it is the book whose copies dominate ancient historical records. In other words, it has the most evidence.

Age of Manuscripts. Another test of a document's reliability is called the *bibliographic test*. This states that the closer a manuscript is written to the time of the events that it describes, the more reliable it is. Now if you have heard that the Bible cannot be trusted because we have no original manuscripts (i.e. Matthew's gospel written by his own hand), this is not fair because *no* original manuscripts exist for *any* ancient document we know about today. All ancient documents are copies.

Therefore, when talking about ancient documents, the bibliographic test looks at how old a copy of a manuscript is, and how far away it is from the events it describes. The newer (or younger) the copy, the further away it is from the original events, so it is less reliable. The older it is, the more reliable it is.

Almost everything we know about the ancient world comes from copies of ancient documents, yet the average copy is often over 1000 years later from the events it describes. For instance, the *Histories* of Herodotus, which was written between 480-425BC, are considered the most reliable account of classical Greece. But not only are there no original manuscripts from Herodotus, the earliest copy we have (of 8 existing ones) is from 900AD—a full 1300 years after he lived.

Similar statistics apply to the writings of Aristotle, the most important Greek philosopher. But no scholar doubts the reliability of Aristotle's philosophy texts. We just assume his writing (and existence) must be more reliable than Jesus' or a Bible author's. Why? Because of the influence of skepticism on our educational institutions.

But the facts say otherwise. For example, the earliest portions of the Gospel of Matthew were written only 20-30 years after Jesus lived, possibly while Paul was still alive. Over 200 existing copies of New Testament manuscripts have been dated earlier than 600AD, with some of them being written as close to 130 years to the original apostles. Compare this to the average secular document, which is 750-1400 years older than its original author.

Herodotus	New Testament
Written originally 480-425BC	Written originally 50-90AD
About events over 1000 years prior to his time.	About events in the preceding 20-90 years
No original manuscripts	No original manuscripts
8 existing copies	24,600 existing copies
Earliest copy: 900AD	Earliest copy: 180AD
Gap: 1400 years	Gap: 130 years

Clearly the standards for trusting secular manuscripts are much lower than the standards for trusting the Bible. If we were to apply a skeptic's standards of "proving" the Bible to any other work in classical antiquity, there would be basically nothing to speak of.

So it's interesting ask, if the New Testament is the most historically reliable document known to humanity, then why do people think it's the least?

OLD TESTAMENT ARCHAEOLOGY

The 1800s was the high point of Bible skepticism. An intellectual movement in Germany, called **Higher Criticism**, led the charge by questioning the authorship and dating of Biblical books. They said Biblical authors didn't exist, or wrote much later than they said they did, or added things to the text to support their opinions and make it seem divine.

The general conclusion was that the Bible was simply a myth—an interesting piece of folklore with complex moral statements—but not about real people in real time. The impression German Higher Criticism made was that Judeo-Christianity was simply a big hoax. Neither the supernatural aspects were true, nor the historical ones, so you were a fool to believe the Bible.

This kind of scholarship circulated universities and tore down the Bible's reputation among educated thinkers. It was largely entrenched before archaeological excavation could prove otherwise.

But as the 1900s progressed, modern Israel became a nation and technology developed. Archaeologists began discovering all kinds of confirming evidence about Biblical places, people, and dates. The field of **Biblical archaeology** was born, and it drove back the accusations of the skeptics.

To date, *no archaeological find has yet disproved any part of the Bible*. This is amazing considering how long a time span the Bible covers and the diversity of cultures it speaks of.

Attacks on Genesis. In the beginning, a lot of scholarly attack was launched against Genesis, the oldest and most foundational book of the Bible. It was assumed that bringing its credibility into question would bring the entire Scripture into question.

Critics claimed Abraham never existed, nor Joseph, nor the early kings, cities, and people groups. Historians said Moses couldn't have written Genesis or the Law because there was not writing back then. Nor was there any proof that the Hebrews were ever in Canaan, or that later, Joshua's military defeated the Canaanites and secured Israel's possession of their land.

It was going to be difficult to prove otherwise because the days of Abraham dated back to at least 2000BC. Very few artifacts could be expected to weather 4000 years of history in the Middle East. Even if they did, there was no certainty that they would have any Biblical relevance, i.e. to validate an account in Genesis. But evidence rolled in!

First the *Nuzi tablets* were found, dating back to the time of Abraham, Isaac, and Jacob. These confirmed dozens of customs in Genesis such as barren wives giving handmaidens to their husbands (as Sarah did with Hagar); a bride being chosen for the son by the father (as Rebekah was); a dowry paid to the father-in-law (as Laban received); work done to pay the dowry (like Jacob did);

birthrights given to the firstborn (as Ishmael, Esau, and Ephraim had); the legality of a blessing given by father to son (as Isaac blessed Jacob, Jacob blessed Ephraim and Manasseh); and more.

Then the *Mari* and *Ebla tablets* were found. These confirmed the existence of cities detailed in early Genesis, including Sodom, Gomorrah, and Zoar. The Ebla tablets were especially interesting because they confirmed that there was indeed systematic writing 500 years before Moses, and that drawing up law codes with judicial proceedings, like Moses did, was normal for a civilization that old.

An Ebla Tablet

Another group of tablets from Egypt did even more that that—they confirmed the existence of a group called the *Habiru* or *'Apiru* (Hebrew) invading Palestine. Their description of turmoil and request for Egyptian troops to help sounded suspiciously like Joshua and the Israelites' invasion. The tablets were dated back to 1500-1400BC, the most commonly proposed time of the Exodus and conquest of Canaan.

Findings which verified Old Testament history continued to be discovered. But even more significantly, *the Bible began to shape the field of archaeology*, even providing a corrective to secular history. For example, most historians and archaeologists didn't believe the Hittites ever lived in Palestine, certainly not in any significant way, and not during the time of Abraham. Some even doubted the Hittites' existed at all, even though the Bible mentions them throughout the Old Testament.

Then archaeologists discovered the Hittites were a major world empire! Today they have substantiated that there were 1200 years of Hittite civilization, much of it corresponding with the time of the Biblical patriarchs.

Old Testament Archaeology		
OT Ref.	Fact in Doubt	Archaeological Proof
Gen. 50:13	Abraham never existed?	Field of Abram mentioned in 918BC by Pharaoh Shishak of Egypt, after he had finished warring with Palestine.
	Genesis names people and places which never existed?	Mari tablets from the Euphrates valley mentions King Arioch (Gen 14) and also lists the towns of Nahor and Harran (Gen. 24:10). Ebla tablets from Syria lists the cities of Sodom, Gomorrah, Admah, Zebolim, and Zoar in the exact sequence of Gen 14.8
	No-one ever mentions ancient Hebrews. They didn't exist at all?	Various Egyptian, Sumerian, Hittite, and Akkadian sources refer to the *Habiru* or *'Apiru*, a group of nomadic invaders who were rebels, mercenaries, laborers in Palestinian territory.
	No such thing as Hittites?	Inscriptions from that period prove that there was 1200 years of Hittite civilization, overlapping with the Jewish patriarchs.
Gen. 36:20	No such thing as Horites?	A mention in the genealogy of Esau, the Horites were discovered as a group of warriors living in Mesopotamia during the patriarchal period.
Gen. 37:28	Joseph's story is fake?	According to trade tablets from that period in Egypt, 20 shekels was the correct price for a slave at that exact time.
Exodus	No evidence of Hebrews in Egypt?	Beni Hasan Tomb from the Abrahamic period depicts people coming west to Egypt during a famine.
	There was no writing during the time of Moses?	The Black Stele was found with Hammurabi's laws, written 300 years before Moses and in the same general region. Later, the Ebla tablets were discovered with writing from even earlier.

Joshua	No evidence of the Hebrews entering Canaan?	The Amarna Tablets from 1500-1400BC speak of an uprising in Palestine by the Habiru with a request for Egyptian troops. Descriptions and timeframe fit the turmoil caused by Joshua and the Israelites invading.
Joshua 6:20	The miracles were all fake?	Excavation at Jericho shows the walls fell outwards as described.
Isaiah 20:1	There was no such king as Sargon II, King of Assyria?	Paul Emil Botta discovered the remains of Sargon II's palace in 1843.
2 Sam. 5:6-10	David uses water shafts built by the Jebusites?	Historians had assumed these were legendary until excavations found on Ophel found them.
Dan. 5	Belshazzar never existed? Instead, Nabodinus was the true king?	In 1854, excavations at Ur showed that Nabodinus delegated power to his oldest son Belshazzar while he was away. He even allowed him the royal title of "King." Interestingly, Daniel 5:29 says Daniel was elevated to "third" place in the kingdom, implying that Belshazzar himself was only second.

A similar thing happened with the existence of the Horites, a tribe that historians also doubted. Archaeology later substantiated their existence as a group of warriors living in Mesopotamia, just as the Bible says.

There are many more instances of Biblical archaeology confirming the Old Testament text, as well as the Old Testament shedding light on archaeological finds. The chart on the preceding pages summarizes just a few major discoveries.

QUESTIONING THE PROPHETS

Besides Biblical history and archaeology, another one of the Bible's most vulnerable points of attack is its claim that the Old Testament prophets were real—that they were actual individuals who supernaturally predicted events which had not happened yet, and which they had no prior knowledge of. In comparison to other documents of the ancient world, the Bible uniquely stakes its reliability on this feature.

Hostile scholars have therefore rightfully discerned that if they can discredit the prophetic aspect of the Bible, which is on display for all to see and makes it stand out in nature and authority among other texts, then they have a foothold in destroying the entirety of Judeo-Christianity.

Not only would discrediting the Prophets destroy belief in the Old Testament, which Judaism and Christianity both rest upon, but they would destroy the notion of the prophetic and the supernatural that is the heart of Jewish and Christian belief... Jesus, for example, came as a fulfillment of (authentic) Old Testament prophecy, claimed to be resurrected, said that people also would rise again, and then prophesied that He would return to start a new heavens and new earth at a God-ordained moment at (a real) end of history. Our hope rests in all these beliefs, by faith in the prophetic and the supernatural.

Incidentally, other world religions including Islam and Mormonism also rely on the prophetic. As spoken by their own prophets, they accept Jesus' existence, the supernatural, and the witness of ancient texts. Destroying the prophetic has therefore been a lynchpin of all who wish to discredit religious belief across the world.

When Higher Criticism popularized criticality of the Biblical text, they accused the prophetic books of being **backdated.** They said the Prophets were not actually predicting future events, but describing *present* or *past* events. Later, books were doctored to appear older and more accurate than they were.

Some also doubted the authorship of the books, saying prophets like Jonah never existed, or that multiple authors were involved. Some said the Old and New Testaments were cobbled together from a variety of unrelated sources that were later edited and ascribed to a prophet. Editors might have even inserted prophecies to make it sound as though it was predicting things that they knew would come to pass later, or fulfilling an action an earlier prophet predicted would happen. As one noted atheist described it,

> "... just like the Old Testament, the "New" one is also a work of crude carpentry, hammered together **long after its purported events**, and full of improvised attempts **to make** things come out right." – Christopher Hitchens, "God is NOT Great: How Religion Poisons Everything"

While unbelievers originally led this bandwagon between approximately 1750-1950, many religious adherents have joined it over time. Those who believe but doubt the historicity of their faith or the supernatural elements have joined secular scholars in trying to discredit the Prophets.

The Reliability of the Prophets

However, by believing these things, those who doubt have had to make up arguments which are often more incredible to believe than just believing in prophecy! In light of the accusations, a number of things can be said in defense of the prophets.

Cultural accuracy. First, prophetic books faithfully reflect the culture and time of their writing, not later ones. If prophetic authors had penned their prophecies later, their style, language, and observations would have been significantly different. For instance, Jeremiah would have used Babylonian expressions if he had written his prophecies about the Babylonian captivity *after* the Babylonians had captured Israel (and him). After 70 years, Jeremiah would have been born, raised, and educated in Babylon, not Israel.

Similar things can be said about Ezekiel, Daniel, and other prophets who all reflect their correct century and location.

High, worldwide stakes. An interesting point about the prophets' reliability is that they predicted events outside Jewish politics, like the fall of the Roman Empire and the Babylonian Captivity. They prophesied major global events that everyone later confirmed really happened.

This is high stakes prophecy, and worldwide in scope. If prophecy had been in the prophets' own mind, rather than in God's mind, they most likely would have restricted themselves to small events that were unprovable or significant only to their own audiences.

But they didn't do this. They prophesied things that would discredit them instantly if they were wrong, such as Israel's invasion by Assyria and Babylon. Records from these major civilizations would have easily proven if the prophets were wrong, and could have discredited them for the rest of history.

The prophets prophesied other incredible things like the destruction of major people groups who were very strong at their time. Nahum prophesied the destruction of Ninevah at the height of Assyria's power. This was illogical also because Jonah had just had success there. Tyre and Sidon were told that they would become a place where fishermen would spread their nets (Ezekiel 26:4-6). Not only did that seem unlikely at the time, but only around 1900AD did the natural disaster occur that made Tyre a place where fishermen hang their nets!

Unpredictable events. Even more amazing are prophecies which predicted the success or downfall of people groups not even *in existence* at the time the prophet lived. For example, Joshua prophesied the destruction of the Philistines, Moabites, and Syrians who didn't exist in his time. Daniel prophesied not just the rise of the Greeks and Romans, but their defeat—when Greece was barely on the map and Rome did not exist yet.

Abraham predicted 400 years of slavery for his people in Egypt before his grandson Jacob was even born. Moses prophesied the exile of Israel into Babylon, 1000 years before it happened. Isaiah prophesied that Cyrus the Great, specifically, would be the one to liberate Israel from exile, more than 100 years before Cyrus was born. These are incredible predictions!

Of course the Jewish prophecies about the Messiah are some of the most amazing because the prophets lived hundreds of years before Christ and had nothing to gain from matching their descriptions to Jesus so well.

For example, Zechariah prophesied that the Messiah would ride a donkey into the Great City (9:9), and that His side would be pierced (12:10). This was more than 400 years before Jesus was born. Isaiah prophesied hundreds of years before that that that the Messiah would be born of a virgin (7:4) and crucified with rebels (53:12) before being buried in a rich man's tomb (53:9). The Psalms prophesied He would be given gall and vinegar to drink, and have lots cast for His clothes (Ps. 22:18, 69:21).

It was prophecies like these that made Bible skeptics first postulate the theory that prophetic books had to be fake and backdated—because the information was so accurate. But the Jews had no motive to be so accurate. Their prophecies point directly to Jesus, whom they don't accept as the Messiah.

Jewish believers today still read the same Old Testament we do and believe those prophecies about the coming Messiah—just not that Christ fulfilled them. So in effect the Jewish faith provides perhaps the most hostile but faithful witness in the case for Christ's existence, and for the reliability of Christianity.

The unity of the message. Biblical prophecies about Israel, the Gentiles, the Messiah, and the Day of the Lord overlap remarkably. Each author has a distinct personality, yet the Bible as a whole has rich literary harmony. Themes which begin in Genesis build all the way to Revelation.

The unity of the prophets' messages over approximately 1000 years, from Moses to Malachi, shows that they were speaking from some common source, i.e. the Holy Spirit. The prophets came from different backgrounds, were different ages, had different intellectual abilities and social standings. Most were separated from each other by centuries.

On a human level, there is no way 1000 years of prophecy could be harmonized like this. Yet the corroboration between prophets is so strong that Bible skeptics have been forced to propose that an individual or small group of individuals must have gone back to write or edit the Old Testament to make it sound so coordinated.

This is quite a claim. It speaks of a conspiracy either among Jews or Christians, or between them, that neither religion would have benefited from. To what credit would it have been for Christians to make the Old Testament sound so solid? Or for Jews, to put so many prophecies of Jesus in it?

The fact is, it would have been extremely controversial for Jews or Christians (or some combination of them) to participate in such a fraud. Pulling it off would have been difficult, a secret that the conspirators would have been put to death for. An even more disturbing implication of this accusation is that the original history and purpose of the Jewish people, as told by the Old Testament, is a lie and had to be made up later by people with an agenda. This is anti-Semitism in barely veiled form.

We should note here that there is no actual evidence for backdating or conspiracy—other than the disbelief in prophecy.

But let's look at a specific example to see how this accusation works. Consider how Daniel 9 prophesies the exact year of Jesus' crucifixion. Because it does, Bible skeptics claim that the Daniel 9 prophecy is fake and was backdated after Jesus was crucified to sound like legitimate prophecy.

But then how did it get (and stay) in the *Jewish* canon of Scripture? Did a Christian go back and insert it? If so, how? Where? Did they attend a rabbinical school undercover, and adulterate an original scroll somewhere?—what about the multiple copies of Daniel that could have corrected this error?

And *when* did they do this? 500 years after Daniel was written, just after Jesus came?—how could they do so, since the Jews were dispersed out of Rome by then? Later, during the Middle Ages?— what about the older copies of the Hebrew Bible that show the prophecy in it, in ancient Hebrew? A Jewish rabbi would not have believed in changing the text, or permitting someone else to do it.

Common sense questioning often reveals major holes in skeptical theories.

The mundane nature of prophecy. The unity of the Old Testament causes problems for some skeptics, yet the disunity causes problems for others. Funnily enough, Old Testament prophecies do not actually appear as though they were edited and backdated later on during a conspiracy. For all their harmony in the big picture, they are diverse and uncoordinated in the details.

For example, many prophecies in the Old Testament are very plain. They were about small things, unimportant people, or events looking ahead only a couple of years. Why have these alongside the bold, explicit, and apocryphal prophecies, unless they were actually for the time being spoken of?

Some prophecies are messy, going on for long numbers of chapters. Others seem abbreviated, with much left out. Still others are vague, and eventually got interpreted with time but confused those who heard initially. Many are still debated, with entire websites devoted to how exactly they were fulfilled. If the prophetic books had been collected and assembled by Jewish or Christian scholars later, they speak of horrible editing!

The sanctity of Scripture. Anyone who glibly says the Old Testament prophesies were made up or backwritten also underestimates the copyist ethic employed by the Jews. The Talmudic and Masoretic school had an ultra-meticulous way of copying the Old Testament manuscript because they believed the actual text, including the paper, was holy. If there was a typo, scribes would copy it. They were not allowed to deviate in the slightest while copying. They looked at each letter individually, and if they made even one error, they burned the entire page they were working on.

Dead Sea Scrolls - Isaiah Scroll

The Dead Sea Scrolls. When the Dead Sea Scrolls were found in 1948, they were the oldest portion of the Old Testament ever found. Some of the copied sections were over 2000 years old. In it, a complete copy of the book of Isaiah verified that our current version of Isaiah had only 13 small errors! Additionally, this Isaiah scroll was 1000 years older than the copy our modern text is based on.

This meant Isaiah's text had barely changed at all in 1000 years. And if it had barely changed in that period of 1000 years, it probably hadn't changed much from when Isaiah first penned it.

Coincidentally, the Isaiah Scroll also proved that Christians had *not* adulterated the Hebrew Bible. They had not inserted Messianic prophecies into the book of Isaiah later on, as accused by skeptics, because this Scroll had been written a century *before* Jesus' birth— before Christianity existed.

Keeping this in mind, some of Isaiah's prophecies are quite validating of Jesus being the Messiah:

- That he would be born to a virgin
- That he would be called "God's Son"
- That he would perform miracles
- That he would be preceded by a messenger

- That he would preach light to the Gentiles
- That he would be spit upon and beaten
- That he would be rejected
- That he would be "numbered with the transgressors"
- That he would die for our sins
- That he would be buried in a rich man's tomb

But if Christians were not guilty of inserting these prophecies into Isaiah, then they were likely not guilty of inserting others such as Daniel 9 either.

Of course, for those who believe the Bible, we were already told to believe in the words of Isaiah and when it was written. Jesus quoted the book of Isaiah during His ministry, and the Ethiopian eunuch was reading a copy of the Isaiah scroll when Phillip visited him in his chariot in Acts 8. This indicates that the Jewish Scriptures were complete prior to the New Testament era, especially the Book of Isaiah which Philip proceeded to explain to the eunuch.

But for skeptics who don't trust the Scriptural account, the Dead Sea Scrolls are irrefutable proof that the Biblical text is trustworthy.

NEW TESTAMENT ARCHAEOLOGY

The New Testament has been equally confirmed by Biblical archaeology. For example, the gospel of Luke and the Book of Acts (both authored by Luke), were ruthlessly attacked by skeptics for many years. Their wrath was particularly aroused over Luke's bold statement that he was a "historian" and wrote his account so that Gentile unbelievers could be persuaded by "the facts" (Luke 1:1-4).

Skeptics tore apart his narrative and claimed Luke's vocabulary was inaccurate for the time period he claimed to write in. The implication was that the gospel was inauthentic and therefore disposable as a witness of Christ.

Just like the attacks against Genesis, however, secular accusation backfired. Closer analysis ended up proving the opposite: that Luke's work was authentic, correctly dated, and impeccably accurate.

One telling example was Luke's usage of the word "proconsul" as the title for the Roman official Gallio in Acts 18:12. This was heavily criticized by secular historians because the first-century Roman historian Pliny never referred to Gallio as "proconsul." This fact alone, they said, proved the writer of Acts wrote his account later, after the first century. Otherwise, he would have been aware of Gallio's true position.

Then the *Delphi Inscription*, dated to 52AD, was recovered. It read, "As Lusius Junius Gallio, my friend and the *proconsul* of Achaia..." Not only did it confirm Luke had used the title correctly, but it was then discovered that Gallio only held this position for one year! Thus the writer of Acts had to have written this verse in or around 52AD, not later, or he would have never known that Gallio was indeed "proconsul." He would have described Gallio the exact same way Pliny had, and thus been contradicted by the archaeological find.

Acts 14:6 was also commonly presented as an example of Luke's historical errors. The verse says Paul and Barnabas "entered" the province of Lyconia when they came to Lystra and Derbe. The problem was that Iconium, the city they had fled from, is also in the province of Lyconia—so they could not have been "entering" a province they were already in.

NT Ref.	Fact in Doubt	Archaeological Proof
Rom. 16:23	Erastus not a treasurer of Corinth?	Confirmed by a pavement found in 1629, bearing his name.
Acts 16:12	"*Meris*" the right word to describe Philippi?	Inscriptions were found that used that very word to describe divisions of a district.

Acts 17:6	"*Politarch*" the right term for the leader of Thessalonica?	19 inscriptions have been found which use this title, 5 of them referring to Thessalonica specifically.
Acts 16:20	"*Praetor*" the right term for ruler of Philippi?	The Romans used this word for magistrates of their own colonies.
Acts 18:12	Gallio really the "*proconsul*" of Lystra?	Delphi inscription calls Gallio "proconsul," a position he only held for one year.
Luke 2:1	Romans did not commonly hold censuses?	Archeology proved the Romans did hold censuses every fourteen years.
Luke 2:3	People did not have to return to their homelands during a census?	A papyrus found in Egypt gave directions for a Roman census and ordered all people who were abroad to come home.
Luke 2:2	Quirinius was governor of Syria at a much later date?	Quirinius was found to be governor of Syria twice—once around 7BC and again around 6AD.

Archaeological evidence eventually showed that Iconium was *not* part of Lyconia between 37-72AD; it had been temporarily made part of Phrygia at that time. Even better, both before 37AD and after 72AD, Iconium *had* been part of Lyconia. So, Luke's testimony was not only correct, but had to have been written in that specific time period as the Bible indicated it was.

This kind of cycle has happened often. The accusations critics think sounds perfect in the beginning turns out to be exactly the opposite: hard evidence they are wrong. The preceding chart summarizes a number of archaeological finds that have supported New Testament dates and history.

Changing stance. Support from archaeology has been so good for the Bible that several archaeologists who entered the field originally skeptical have come out convinced believers.

Sir William Ramsey

One of them, Sir William M. Ramsey, became one of Biblical archaeology's founding fathers. Rising through the British Academy in Oxford, he received honorary degrees and memberships in every area of archeology, geography, and historical research. He was eventually knighted and given an award by the Pope. By his death in 1906, he had concluded that both the New Testament and the gospel author Luke were undoubtedly accurate, saying:

"Luke is a historian of the first rank. Not merely are his statements of fact trustworthy...this author should be placed along with the very greatest historians."

Proving Luke's accuracy, or the accuracy of any other New Testament writer, does not prove the gospel is from God. But it at least establishes that the Bible is genuine and historical, not full of errors and mythology. Nor was it backdated by Christians in later centuries just to make their religion sound more legitimate, as has been accused of them.

Believers need to know that in the last 150 years or so, enough ancient excavation been done to really authenticate the Old and New Testament texts. It has provided background to Biblical history, confirmed contexts and geographical locations, filled out Biblical stories, and helped resolve difficult passages.

It has also confirmed the historicity of the patriarchs, the Jewish Law, wars, prophecies, New Testament disciples, and locations of missions. The fact is, that if the Bible were fraudulent, there would be no reason for Jewish and Christian people to exist, let alone all the copies of ancient gospels and epistles, or the temples and churches of old. Archaeology demands an explanation for these things.

In conclusion, for those who maintain that the Bible is a myth, archaeology is one field you can point to that scientifically upholds the Bible's authenticity and accuracy.

Tacitus, Roman historian

HISTORICAL WITNESSES OF THE NEW TESTAMENT

History is another field that validates the Bible. Many people do not realize there are historical witnesses who testify that Jesus Christ existed. They think the Bible is the only source that says Christ and Christianity existed. That isn't true.

One of the most important corroborations of Jesus' life is found in the writing of the official Roman (non-Christian) historian, Tacitus. He lived from 55-117AD and testified that Jesus died under Pontius Pilate, as it is told in the Bible. In his *Annals of History*, he wrote:

> Hence to suppress the rumor, he [Caesar] falsely charged with the guilt, and punished with the most exquisite tortures, the persons commonly called Christians, who were hated for their enormities. Christos [Christ], the founder of the name, was put to death by Pontius Pilate, procurator of Judea in the reign of Tiberius; but the pernicious superstition, repressed for a time broke out again, not only through Judea, where the mischief originated, but through the city of Rome also (Annals XV .44).

Tacitus' testimony here is very important because he confirms basic facts from the New Testament including the persecution of Christians, Jesus as the founder, Pilate's official position, Judea as the place of origin, etc. Yet Tacitus had no motive to corroborate the New Testament account. He wasn't a Christian, and the early Romans persecuted the Church—they had no reason to give credence to Christ. Even Tacitus' use of a slightly incorrect version of Jesus' name ("Christos") confirms this is an authentic text, not a doctored one for an ulterior motive—a popular charge by skeptics.

Another historian, the first-century Jewish scholar Josephus, also confirms Jesus' life and death. His account confirms several key parts of the gospel:

> There was about this time Jesus, a wise man...He drew over to him many of the Jews and many of the Gentiles. He was Christ; and when Pilate, at the suggestion of the principal men amongst us, had condemned him to the Cross, those that loved him at the first did not forsake him, for he appeared to them alive again the third day...and the tribe of Christians, so named from, are not extinct at this day. (Antiq. XVIII 3:3)

The reliability of this particular passage in Josephus' history is sometimes disputed because parts of the phraseology seem too approving of Jesus for someone who was Jewish. Many believe the passage was embellished as it passed through the hands Christian monks who transcribed Josephus' works in the Middle Ages. Yet it is unlikely the passage itself is fabrication because Josephus mentions Jesus in other places in his text, as well as John the Baptist, James the apostle, and the Sanhedrin (i.e. Antiquities XX 9:1).

The important thing is that first-hand corroborations of Jesus' life do exist, from historians who are considered very reliable on other matters. They exist even from non-Christian witnesses who did not benefit from these reports.

CONCLUSION

If internal and external evidence confirm the Bible's reliability and its claims, why do so many people still doubt? The long history of philosophy has proven that anything can be doubted. Everything you think is true can be doubted if you question it enough. You can even doubt your own existence, which is probably the plainest truth you can prove.

This means that there will always be questions about whether or not the God of the Bible is true. If you cannot prove to someone that you exist, you certainly cannot prove that God does. And even though there is a great deal of evidence for the Bible's reliability, there will always be areas where there is no corresponding archaeological record, or where a counterargument seems compelling.

Those who have an axe to grind against the idea of a divinely inspired text, of course go on the attack in just these areas. The important thing for believers to know is that, after centuries of intense criticism, the Bible has shown itself over and over to be worthy of its claim as God's message to humanity. Doubters will go on doubting, but close analysis shows the doubts to be paper thin, not your faith.

Chapter 3:
How We Got the Bible

The Bible is an awesome book. Actually, it is a collection of books. It is a compilation from approximately 40 different authors from different time periods and locations. It was written over a 1500-year period.

But if it was built this way, over such a long period of time, how did it become the final version we have today? And how can we be sure that it is just the way God wants it?

How The Old Testament Came to Be

The story of writing the Bible begins around 1500BC with its first author, Moses. He spent an intense amount of time with God on Mount Sinai. Meeting face to face with the Father, he received an inspired version of ancient history, as well as a divine law code for Israel to live by. Moses then wrote everything down as the first five books of the Bible, which the Hebrews called the **Torah** and the Greeks called the **Pentateuch** ("*penta-*" meaning "five").

As Israel grew and time passed, God inspired other Jewish leaders to write Scripture, including Joshua, Samuel, David, Solomon, Ezra, and the prophets. Their revelations and testimonies were carefully recorded and copied by priests and scribes who used incredibly meticulous processes. The last Old Testament author, Malachi, penned his book around 400BC. Then God closed His written revelation to the Jews.

Canonization of the Old Testament

Around this time, the Old Testament was ***canonized***, or gathered together and made official. For almost 2400 years now, the

Hebrew Bible has consisted of our Old Testament (in Hebrew, and some Aramaic) and is called the **Tanakh**.

Canonization of the Old Testament was relatively easy because the Jews have guarded their Scripture well ever since Moses commanded that they should. The Book of Deuteronomy warned against adding or subtracting from the Scriptures, and Jewish scribes were trained not to lose things, copy inaccurately, or add their own embellishments.

The standard method of copying Scripture was methodical, to guard against corrupting the text. The Talmudic process of copying included rules about how the copyist should sit, what ink he should use, and the instruction that "No word or letter, not even a *yod* [the smallest letter], must be written from memory, the scribe not having looked at the Codex before him."

This meant copyists had to copy mark by mark, extremely slowly. Pages were burnt if they were found to have even one difference from the original. This painstaking process ensured remarkable accuracy, and the result was the **Masoretic Text**—the authoritative Hebrew text of the Jewish Bible today. This format was completed in the 7th century AD (600s) and has been widely copied and distributed. It is very close to some of our oldest copies of the *Tanakh*.

Also contributing to the stability of the Old Testament was the fact that Scriptures were discussed publicly in **synagogues** starting around 400BC, when the Second Temple was established in Jerusalem. In synagogues, teachers read aloud from the scrolls and interpreted the text. It was at this time when teaching became an established profession in Israel, and rabbinical schools of thought developed around different teaching traditions. Some of the oldest copies we have today of the Hebrew Bible date back to this era, around 200 years before Christ.

It should be obvious, then, that Bible skeptics' accusation that the Old Testament wasn't codified until after Jesus' birth, makes no sense with Jewish history. The Old Testament was in complete form, publicly, well before the time of Jesus.

JESUS UPHOLDS THE OLD TESTAMENT

Jesus upheld this accurate, canonized status of the Old Testament. He taught Scripture (the Old Testament) to Hebrew Bible teachers in the Temple when He was a boy. He also taught His disciples on the road to Emmaus after He rose again:

> "Beginning with Moses and with all the Prophets, He explained to them the things concerning Himself in all the Scriptures." (Luke 24:27).

Throughout the New Testament, Jesus' continual referral to the Old Testament as "the Law and the Prophets" indicates that Jewish consensus on what was divine text was well understood. Jesus never corrected Jewish leaders for having anything wrong or missing from their Scriptures, which He certainly would have done if there had been corruption at that time.

For their part, the Pharisees attacked Jesus on many fronts, but they never argued over whether a verse He was citing was Scripture or not—they contested only His interpretations and applications of verses.

Most experts agree that Jesus quoted 24 books of the Old Testament, and that the New Testament quotes 34 of them, while alluding to all 39—upholding the Old Testament's status as canonized and accurate at the time of Jesus.

HOW THE NEW TESTAMENT CAME TO BE

Most of the Old Testament was written in Hebrew, but after the Greeks conquered Palestine in 332BC, the Old Testament was translated into a Greek version known as the **Septuagint**. This would later be used by the Greek-speaking Church as the basis of their Old Testament (rather than the Hebrew).

The New Testament authors themselves also wrote in Greek. This was significant because rather than write in the language of the Hebrews, who had been the focus of the Old Testament, God chose to have the apostles (who could have written in Hebrew) write in the common language of the world at that time. The language change of the New Testament therefore reflected God's change in focus, from one people group to the people of the entire world.

The entire New Testament was written in a very short period of time, between 50-100AD, by Paul and apostles who walked with Christ. Even before it was finished, false teachings started permeating the Church. Even as John the apostle was writing the very last books, false gospels and epistles were being written which mixed Greek philosophy with Christianity.

There began to be a need to separate wheat from chaff, and close the canon. It was for this reason that as soon as Christianity became legalized in the 4th century AD, the Church officially named the list of books which were authoritative—our current New Testament.

THE CANONIZATION PROCESS OF THE NEW TESTAMENT

But could a search for what belongs in the canon be reliable? Especially if it was 300 years after Jesus...how do we know the Church was accurate? It's easy, from a modern perspective, to view the canonization process as unreliable. It seems like an ancient relic of Catholic history.

To some extent, there is faith involved. You have to believe that God and the Holy Spirit were involved in the Church Fathers' examination into what was inspired and what wasn't. You have to trust that the Holy Spirit guided that process just as He guided the original authorship. You have to believe that God was still invested in protecting His message, just as He was during the Old Testament period.

However, your confidence can be based on more than just faith. Canonization was not a chaotic process of compiling lots of purported scriptures and then trying to figure out which ones belonged. It was a scientific process which confirmed books that had been in use in churches from the beginning—books that had a clear factual and historical account of Jesus, as well as a direct connection to the original apostles.

New Testament books had to pass four tests: 1) apostolicity, 2) large-scale acceptance by the Church, 3) orthodoxy, and 4) edification or quality of inspiration. The approach was not, "What books can we proxy into Scripture, like the Gospel of Thomas?" but "What books do we have that everyone recognizes and is using already?"

When Bible conspiracy theorists talk about the Bible, they argue that there were many viable candidates the Church Fathers rejected—the Gospel of Thomas, the Gospel of Judas, 1 and 2 Enoch, etc. In reality, there was great agreement among Christians in the early 300s about what Scripture included and what it didn't.

For example, the apostle John lived until almost 100AD, so he was an authoritative presence up until that point. He also had direct disciples involved in the earliest part of the New Testament collection process.

The first gospels, known as the "Memoirs of the Apostles," were widely passed around prior to 100AD. Copies of Paul's epistles were also circulating churches by the end of the 100s, and were the first to be collected, by leaders at Ephesus who had been instructed by Paul personally.

The following table summarizes how the New Testament got into its final form:

Church Father	Date	NT Books Recognized
John (Jesus' disciple)	90-95AD	Wrote 1-3 John, and the Book of Revelation
Clement of Rome	95	8 books
Polycarp (John's disciple)	108	15 books
Muratorian Council	180	22 books
Irenaeus	185	21 books
Hippolytus	235	22 books
Origen	200	23 books
Eusebius	325	20 books
Athanasius	367	27 books

The Church Fathers quickly affirmed most of the New Testament books—21 of them had been proven reliable by the period of John's disciples. It took longer to confirm the remaining 6 books— James, 2 Peter, 2 and 3 John, Jude, Hebrews, and Revelation— because they wanted to make sure they were clearly connected to apostolic authors.

Sometimes this slow process is seen as a reason we should distrust canonization. But the church leaders knew they were building the foundation of Christian civilization. We should respect their caution, especially considering how heretical things were in their day, and how there was no public information to work off of—no seminaries, no commentaries, no museums or libraries.

The public announcement in the early 300s was therefore not a random, Catholic creation. It is not as if Jesus died in 33AD and then, suddenly 300 years later, a council of removed, unbelieving men tried to piece together the New Testament. There were many active disciples and scholars working on the canonization process prior to its final form in 325AD. It just could not get the finances, resources, and things it needed until Christianity was legalized and publicly commissioned.

Some still ask, but why did the process of canonization have to take place at all? The simplest answer is, to preserve the message. By

100AD, all the original apostles had died and direct ties to them were going to disappear. It became increasingly important that the information "everyone knew" be formally consolidated and recognized for future generations.

Already, false books had been written, and some sects were writing new ones. Some believed God would keep revealing new Scripture down through the ages. By the 300s, when the Roman Empire became officially Christian, the Church Fathers were convinced the canon was closed and wanted to officially sound that trumpet. They knew any forthcoming revelation would not be on the same plane as the original apostles who had direct ties to Jesus.

So those who think the canonization process corrupted the message of the Bible have it backwards. The process confirmed and preserved the message from future corruption.

Thankfully, the Church Fathers were a very reputable group of men. What they did was not altogether new. God has used councils of men to govern His Church since the very beginning, and through to this day. The Jews started this tradition through the Sanhedrin, a group of elders who legally guarded the Scripture and debated interpretations of it in the Old Testament era.

In the New Testament era, the first council took place in Jerusalem when the elders debated Paul over the issue of circumcision for believers in Acts 15. Councils continued down through the first, second, and third centuries to discuss issues and doctrines important to the Church. After a series of them in the 300s, all the researchers affirmed that only the 27 current books of the New Testament were apostolic. Many believing bishops and scholars had a pivotal role in these councils, including Saint Augustine who was one of the most brilliant minds Western civilization has ever seen.

Those who think councils were manmade foolishness, perhaps invented by the Catholics or controlled by the Pope, are wrong.

They were invented by God in the Biblical account, and were quite democratic for their time.

THE REFORMATION

After all this work, a new Bible translation was needed. Latin was the common language of the Roman Empire, not Greek. The Church needed a new authoritative version of the Bible once the canonization process ended.

The government commissioned one of the Church Fathers, Jerome, to write a Latin translation that would take into account the conclusions of the councils. Jerome's translation became known as the **Vulgate** (from *"vulga-"* meaning "common"). It became the official translation for the Catholic Church, from approximately 400AD down through the Middle Ages.

The Vulgate was good for Jerome's time but within 200 years, the Roman church declared that the Bible could only be used in Latin. This caused a problem. As Christianity grew during the Middle Ages, it started incorporating all different groups of people and languages. It was no longer a small church centered around Rome, but a diverse faith scattered across Europe, the Middle East, and Asia Minor.

The Scriptures eventually became imprisoned in a language not used by most people. Even worse, through hundreds of years of use and abuse by political figures, the Vulgate's text got corrupted. There was no way to copy or print the text the Church did have, across its wide territory. Knowledge of the Bible became increasingly rare, even among priests, bishops and theologians.

Suddenly, in 1384, **John Wycliffe** translated the Bible into the language of the common people of England! This made him infamous throughout Europe. The Pope was so infuriated that 44 years after Wycliffe's death, he had Wycliffe's bones dug up, crushed, and scattered.

Jan Hus, a Czech scholar, then picked up the work of Wycliffe in his native land. His reward was to be burned at the stake in 1415 with Wycliffe's Bibles used as kindling for the fire. His dying words were, "In 100 years, God will raise up a man whose calls for reform cannot be suppressed." Martin Luther's reforms began almost exactly 100 years later.

In the meantime, the invention of the printing press by Johannes Gutenberg in 1440 made it possible for the first time to produce many copies of a book at a rapid pace, instead of spending years copying it by hand. The first book to be printed on it was... a Bible! But it was still in Latin, a language only understood by priests.

At the same time, in 1453, the fall of Constantinople to the Muslims led many Greek Christians to flee to Western Europe, with their copies of ancient Greek manuscripts. This led to a revival of interest in the original Greek Scriptures, and sparked the Protestant Reformation.

Scholars began to learn Greek to read the original manuscripts. One Englishman, John Colet, began to read the New Testament in Greek and translate passages into English for his sermons. People were so hungry to hear the real Word of God that within six months, 20,000 people packed into St. Paul's Cathedral in London with about as many outside trying to get in. Only Colet's connections in very high places kept him from execution.

Another Englishman, Thomas Linacre, was an Oxford professor who learned Greek just to read the original Biblical texts. Afterwards, he made this striking comment: "Either this (the original Greek) is not the gospel, or we are not Christians." Clearly, Latin was not the language of the common people anymore, and the Latin Bible had been corrupted to the point that the gospel was obscured.

Meanwhile, for political reasons, the Pope began threatening to execute anyone who read the Scripture in any other language than Latin. Foxe's Book of Martyrs records that in 1517, seven people were burned at the stake simply for teaching their children to say the Lord's Prayer in English, rather than Latin.

Thomas Linacre had a student named Erasmus, a Catholic scholar who used the best sources he could find to produce a whole Greek New Testament. It suddenly became available to all who were interested in what the Scripture sounded like prior to 1000 years of Latin captivity. Erasmus hoped that the Greek Scriptures would help reform the Catholic church, but it ended up fueling the Protestant Reformation instead. The Pope condemned him for producing a "fable of Christ" for profit.

Meanwhile, Reformers such as Martin Luther and William Tyndale quickly picked up Erasmus' Greek translation.

Martin Luther began the **Protestant Reformation** of the church in 1517. He emphasized the importance of justification by faith instead of works. He also condemned the Roman Catholic church for indulgences and corrupt interpretations of the Bible.

By 1522, Luther had translated the New Testament from Greek into German. By the 1530s he had a complete Bible in his native tongue. For the first time in almost 1000 years, the Bible had been returned to a language of common people. Germans rejoiced, and the Reformation grew there.

Meanwhile, **William Tyndale**, a scholar who knew eight languages and wanted to translate the Bible into English, was the first to print an English New Testament based on the original Greek. He fled England when bounty hunters and Inquisitors came after him. For eleven years, they hunted him, constantly on his trail to arrest him and prevent the printing of the Bible in a common language.

Tyndale arrived in Germany in 1525 and, within a year, an English New Testament was being printed there. Copies were smuggled into England through bales of cotton and sacks of flour. Those who were caught with Tyndale's Bible could be burned at the stake. But the more the King of England condemned it, the more fascinated everyone became with it.

In retaliation, the Catholic church accused Tyndale of making thousands of errors, but they burned his Bible because they could find no errors at all! Because it was fueling the Reformation, they began buying up copies of his Bible to burn them. But Tyndale used the money to print even more.

Copies of the Tyndale Bible were burned as soon as the Bishop of England could confiscate them, but somehow, a copy fell through and ended up in the bedroom of King Henry VIII. God was moving.

Tyndale was eventually caught when a friend betrayed him, and he was jailed for 500 days, strangled, then burned at the stake in 1536. His last words were, "Oh Lord, open the King of England's eyes." Three years later, his prayer was answered when Henry VIII funded his own printing of an English Bible called **The Great Bible,** largely based on Tyndale's work.

The battle for the Scriptures in English continued through the work of Miles Coverdale, who published the first full English Bible while Tyndale was in prison, in 1535. In 1540, Coverdale worked with the Archbishop of Canterbury, Thomas Cranmer, to publish Henry VIII's Great Bible and have one chained to every pulpit in England so citizens could have access to it.

But in 1555, when Queen "Bloody" Mary took the throne, Archbishop Cranmer was tried and forced to sign a recantation of his work. He was supposed to preach a sermon on the day of his execution that admitted to his "crimes," but in the middle of the sermon, he gained courage and took back his recanting. Before he could be pulled down off the pulpit, he said of the signed deed: "This was the hand that wrote it; therefore it shall suffer first punishment." His hand was first to be burned in the fire at the stake.

Just after this, the *Geneva Bible* was published from exile in Switzerland. It was also largely based on Tyndale's work and became the favorite Bible of the Puritans and Reformers for the next 200 years. It was even taken to Jamestown and Plymouth in the early 1600s. It had radical anti-Catholic notes in it, so it was hated by King James I who was sympathetic to his Catholic constituency. He published the King James Bible in 1611 as a way of replacing it, which is still one of the most famous versions of the Bible today.

THE BIBLE REGAINS ITS PLACE

By this time, the battle for Scripture in European languages had been won. Catholics published their own Bible translation in the late 1500s to fight the Reformation, but there was no going back to Latin. The great quest for the Bible in the hands of common people was dramatically summed up by the preaching of the great Puritan, "Roaring" John Rogers, who addressed what he saw as lukewarm thankfulness for it as early as 1620:

> First, he [Rogers] portrayed God addressing the congregation and saying: "I have trusted you so long with my Bible, but you have slighted it: it lies in your houses covered over with cobwebs, you care not to listen to it. Because of this you shall have my Bible no longer."

> Removing the huge pulpit Bible from its place, he covered it over with a cloth, then kneeling down in the pulpit he impersonated the people crying: "Oh God, whatever you do, don't take the Bible away from us! Take our children, burn our houses, destroy our goods, but spare us the Bible!"

> Then, acting as God again, he said: "Say you so? Well, I will try you a little while longer." Replacing the Bible onto the reading desk, he said: "I will see from now on how you use it, whether you love it more, observe it more, practice it more, and live more according to it."

> The result of this? The whole congregation dissolved in tears. Thomas Goodwin, who was an eyewitness to this occasion, said that he was compelled to hang for a quarter of an hour upon the neck of

his horse weeping before he had power to mount, so strange an impression was there upon him and generally upon the people.

John Rogers had touched upon a very sensitive spot, for Puritanism, whatever its flaws, was at heart, a Bible movement. The Puritans saw reverence of God as reverence for his Word, and service for God as acting on His Word. They viewed disregarding Scripture as the greatest possible insult to the divine Author.

Part of what makes the United States unique is that we were founded on this sentiment. In the 1600-1700s, Puritans and other Reformers initiated the politics and culture of our nation on believing the Bible and applying Biblical principles. Americans from the beginning were bent towards loving freedom, God, goodness, and progress. They got to skip the 1000 years of church history that was fought from the wilderness, over simply obtaining and distributing an accurate Bible.

We should keep this in mind if we feel critical of the Church's past, or our religious heritage as Americans. It is easy to criticize people, denominations, and beliefs from centuries ago, but our ancestors fought through a lot on faith. The Bible-loving foundation of Protestantism which we all have today is primarily due to them, and their blood, sweat, and tears.

BIBLE TRANSLATION CONTINUES

God began the next phase of Bible history in 1629 when the Bible was translated into the language of the Malay people. In 1662, the great Puritan John Eliot published a Bible in the Algonquin language and discipled what came to be known as the "Praying Tribes" of Massachusetts.

By 1800 there were as many as 50 different translations of the Bible, which ignited the great era of missions. Translation began at full speed.

William Carey sponsored the Bible in 45-60 languages. Adoniram Judson translated the Bible into Burmese in 1816—and invented an alphabet to do it. Henry Martin translated Scripture into Arabic and Persian. By the early 1900s, translations had been done in all the major languages of the world.

Many minor languages were still left. William Cameron Townsend, after trying to reach a native tribe in Central America, found there were many Spanish dialects which had still not been translated. He launched what has become known as the Wycliffe Bible Translators. Their goal is still to translate Scripture into every language in the world.

Also during the 19th century, new ancient manuscripts started being discovered through archaeological excavation. One was even found in a wastebasket in a monastery at the foot of Mount Sinai!

St. Catherine's Monastery

New scientific methods were applied to the ancient manuscripts to discover which texts were the most original. A number of minor changes to the King James text were made, and some verses removed, to reflect the most recent discoveries. A new version of the Bible was published as the Revised Version in England (RV) and the American Standard Version (ASV) in the United States. All modern Bible translations today trace back to this new "critical text," of which there is very high confidence that it is very near the original manuscripts inspired by God.

WHICH BIBLE TO USE?

Ironically, after many centuries of warfare to make the Bible available to the common man, those of us reading in English are now fortunate enough to be faced with a completely new problem:

figuring out *which* Bible is best to use! We now have so many Bibles to choose from that the options can almost be dizzying.

In our opinion, some good choices for reading through the Bible are:

- NIV- the New International Version
- NLT- the New Living Translation
- The Passion Translation
- The Message (a paraphrase)

Some good choices for in-depth Bible studying are:

- NASB- the New American Standard Bible
- ESV- the English Standard Version
- The Amplified Bible
- NKJV- the New King James Version

The thing to keep in mind when considering Bible translations is that the very most important translation is the one that happens between the text and your own heart. The Pharisees had excellent manuscripts and knowledge of the Scripture, but the way their hearts received the Word led them into bondage.

So while we of course want the most accurate Bible we can get, it is important to steer clear from those obsessed with the text and having a "perfect" translation. This is a distraction with no end. We all need to be encouraged to spend the most time meditating on the meaning of Scripture and applying it to our lives, rather than wondering how, for example, certain Greek words are translated.

If you find yourself in a stream that exalts the amount of time you spend with the text, or knowing *about* the text, refresh yourself with Jesus' centered advice that "...these are the very words that testify of *Me*." (John 5:39).

~ Part II ~
What's in the Bible?

Chapter 4:
Structure & Content

The Bible is a collection of 66 smaller books. When you look at your Bible's table of contents and read through the list, it is easy to think these books are just a random assortment of strange-sounding names! It is not apparent, at first glance, that there is any kind of structure.

But God is an intelligent designer. He has intelligently designed the natural world, and He has intelligently designed His Word.

There are different categories of books in the Bible—different *genres*, or types—with different features. These shed light on their purpose and how they should be interpreted. Many times, a passage of Scripture can tell us something simply by where it is in the Bible. When you come across a genealogy, or a narrative, or a prophecy, you can get more meaning out of it because you know the purpose of the different sections.

Recognizing the different genres also helps you develop accurate doctrine. Many people who are unaware of historical or theological context end up using verses in a haphazard way. They may proof-text what they believe with random Scriptures. But good Spirit-led interpretation starts with understanding what the Bible contains and what meaning each section contributes in terms of the whole story.

OLD TESTAMENT STRUCTURE

The Old Testament breaks down into five genres: Law, History, Wisdom, Major Prophets, and Minor Prophets.

Structure of the Old Testament				
Law (5 books)	History (12 books)	Wisdom (5 books)	Major Prophets (5 books)	Minor Prophets (12 books)
Genesis	Joshua	Job	Isaiah	Hosea
Exodus	Judges	Psalms	Jeremiah	Joel
Leviticus	Ruth	Proverbs	Lamentations	Amos
Numbers	1 Samuel	Ecclesiastes	Ezekiel	Obadiah
Deuteron.	2 Samuel	Song of	Daniel	Jonah
	1 Kings	Solomon		Micah
	2 Kings			Nahum
	1 Chron.			Habbakuk
	2 Chron.			Zechariah
	Ezra			Haggai
	Nehemiah			Zephaniah
	Esther			Malachi

You can see that three of the Old Testament categories have five books each, and the other two categories have twelve. There are 39 books of the Old Testament altogether.

The books within each category are in chronological order, with just a few exceptions. This means Genesis is the oldest of the Law books and Deuteronomy is the most recent; Joshua is the first history book of Israel, while Esther is the last; and so forth.

The New Testament is structured differently from the Old Testament. Its books break down into six categories, and they are not in chronological order. Here are the 27 New Testament books, organized by genre:

Structure of the New Testament					
Gospels	**History**	**Letters to Churches**	**Letters to Pastors**	**Letters to All**	**Prophecy**
Matthew Mark Luke John	Acts	Romans 1 Corinth. 2 Corinth. Galatians Ephesians Philippians Colossians 1 Thess. 2 Thess.	1 Tim. 2 Tim. Titus Philemon	Hebrews James 1 Peter 2 Peter 1 John 2 John 3 John Jude	Revelation

Contained in the three "Letters" categories of the New Testament are 21 *epistles* (Greek: *letters*). These are written by apostles who were eyewitnesses to Jesus' ministry. Each epistle category starts with the *longest* letter and ends with the *shortest* one, so Romans is the longest letter to the churches while 2 Thessalonians is the shortest; 1 Timothy is the longest letter to pastors while Philemon is the shortest, etc.

If you can stretch your schema to see the "Gospels" as similar to the Old Testament "Law" books, and the three "Letters" categories as corresponding to the Old Testament "Wisdom" books, then the Old and New Testaments parallel each other quite well. On the following page, you can see how the categories are similar and in the same kind of order.

Each testament begins with Law/History which give the historical foundations of God's people and the principles He wants them to use. Then come Wisdom/Prophecy books which are Spirit-filled messages written by key people the Lord is using at that particular time.

Function	Old Testament	New Testament
Foundations	The five Law books	The four Gospels
Demonstration	OT History books	Book of Acts
Application	Wisdom books	Letters to churches, individuals, and all nations
Predictions	Major Prophets Minor Prophets	Book of Revelation

Each testament moves the reader through foundational ideas, how those ideas played out in real time, theological principles for application, and predictions for the part of God's plan still coming.

When you read the Bible then, the first thing you should think about is what *kind* of book you are reading—history, wisdom, prophets, epistles? Each of the different kinds of books have passages that should be interpreted and applied differently. We will explore this more in the last section of the book, about **hermeneutics**, or principles of interpreting the text.

THE BIBLE'S CHRONOLOGY

After analyzing what genre you are in, another helpful thing to do is analyze the Bible's chronology—the date in which the books were *set*. Note that this may be different from the time that the author actually penned the books. For example, Moses wrote the book of Genesis around 1500BC, but the events he describes in Genesis occurred hundreds or thousands of years before he was born. The following table lists the books of the Old Testament by the time period they were *describing*, or writing about.

Time Period	Law and History	Wisdom	Major Prophets	Minor Prophets
Creation to Exodus (??-1500 BC)	Genesis	Job		
Founding of Israel (ca. 1500-1050 BC)	Exodus Leviticus Numbers Deuteron. Judges Ruth			
United Kingdom (ca. 1050-930 BC)	1 Samuel 2 Samuel 1 Chron.	Psalms Proverbs Eccles. S. of Sol.		
Divided Kingdom (ca. 930-586 BC)	1 Kings 2 Chron 2 Kings		Isaiah	Hosea Joel? Amos Jonah Micah Nahum Habakkuk Zephaniah
Exile/ Captivity (586-520 BC)			Jeremiah Lament. Ezekiel Daniel	Obadiah
Post-Exile (ca.520-400 BC)	Esther Ezra Nehemiah			Haggai Zechariah Joel? Malachi

Some things to notice here include that the first wisdom book, Job, was describing a period of time contemporaneous with Abraham— not David and Solomon's reign like the other wisdom books. In fact, while Genesis describes events prior to Job, Job is commonly said to be the oldest book of the Bible, written at least 500 years before Moses authored Genesis.

Additionally, you can see that the history books run throughout the length of Israel's existence, with a break during the Babylonian exile. The last three history books of Israel—Esther, Ezra, and Nehemiah—pick up where the exile history left off and describe events contemporaneous with the last minor prophets. This history ends around 400BC. In total, Israel's organized history is about 1100 years from 1500BC to 400BC.

Only one major prophet writes in the early days of the monarchy, and that is Isaiah. He overlaps most of the minor prophets. Alternately, only one minor prophet writes during the exile, and that is Obadiah. He overlaps the other major prophets. All the prophets write after the Kingdom of Israel is divided.

Malachi is the last authored book of the Old Testament. Ezra and Nehemiah finish up the history. The last prophets and history books finish up the story of what God is doing and saying about the future while Israel is trying to restore itself.

This next table shows the same kind of chronological breakdown for the books of the New Testament: Looking at this chart, we notice that while many Biblical books are named after the authors who wrote them—Ezra wrote Ezra, Isaiah wrote Isaiah, etc—in the New Testament, only some of them are. Paul's epistles are named after the people who *received* the book, those whom the book was written to. So Galatians was written to the church at Galatia, 1 Timothy was written to Timothy, etc.

Time Period	Gospels/ History	Letters to Churches	Letters to Pastors	Letters to All	Prophecy
Life of Jesus (ca.0-33 AD)	Mark Matthew Luke John				
Early Church (ca. 33-70 AD)	Acts	Galatians 1 Thess. 2 Thess. 1 Corinth. 2 Corinth. Romans Ephesians Colossians Philippians	Philemon 1 Timothy Titus 2 Timothy	James Hebr. 1 Peter 2 Peter Jude	
Church Age (after 70AD)				1 John 2 John 3 John	Revelation

It's also important to realize that when the New Testament authors wrote their portion of Scripture, they were all doing so in roughly the same time period, in the time between 50-95AD. This means they had little access to New Testament material which had been written before them. For example, Matthew did not have access to the letters of Paul as he wrote his gospel. It was only after the entire New Testament had been completed that diverse letters were gathered together and understood to be a collection of revelations which should accompany the Old Testament.

Likewise, while the New Testament was being written, only the Old Testament or "the Law and the Prophets" as Jesus called it, was considered "Scripture." While King David and the Prophets were writing, only the Law was considered Scripture. And while Moses was writing, there was no Scripture! Nothing for him to look back on.

This is important to understand because it acknowledges the role of the Holy Spirit who penned all these books over the centuries. While there were a few occasions where Biblical authors displayed some knowledge of one another, generally "the Bible" as we know it was not formulated until later. Each author had to write with the revelation they got, hoping it would make sense in the entire corpus later.

It is not even clear if each author *knew* how important what they were writing really was, and that what they were contributing would go into a canon of holy Scripture passed down to thousands of years of followers to come!

BIBLE AUTHORS

Approximately 40 followers of God were chosen by Him to write Scripture. The way they did it was through the prompting of the Holy Spirit. The Spirit moved authors to prophesy, to write history prophetically, to make laws, to give eyewitness accounts, to give principles and wisdom through the Spirit, and to write psalms, hymns, and spiritual songs.

Believe it or not, some authors of the Bible remain unknown! No-one has ever pinpointed the author of Job, and discussion is considerable on Joshua, Judges, Ruth, Esther, 1 and 2 Kings, and Hebrews. A few others have portions which are debated. Authorship has always been a tricky issue, but there are significant traditions behind most questions which have not been fully resolved.

It's also important to realize that one book may have several contributors. Psalms and Proverbs stand out noticeably in this category, but other books are joint efforts as well.

Author	Books Written	Possibly wrote
Moses	Genesis, Exodus, Leviticus, Deuteronomy	
Samuel	1 and 2 Samuel	Joshua, Judges, Ruth
David	Psalms (about half)	Ruth
Solomon	Proverbs (more than half), Ecclesiastes, Song of Solomon	Ruth
Jeremiah	Jeremiah Lamentations	1 and 2 Kings
Ezra	1 and 2 Chronicles Ezra	
Luke	Luke, Acts	
Paul	Romans, Galatians, Ephesians,	Hebrews
John	Gospel of John; 1, 2, 3 John, Revelation	Hebrews

For these reasons and more, internet charts of Bible books with their corresponding authors can be lengthy and disagree with one another. Suffice it to say that if you find information where the list of authors is exceedingly long, the Prophets are not assigned the correct Biblical books bearing their name, or multiple authors are assigned to them, or large numbers of questions marks are included in the list of authors, then you are looking at misleading information. Those are normally made by those who do not accept the Bible at face value. They may believe in backdating, conspiracy theories, or the otherwise inauthenticity of the Scripture.

To keep things simple, in addition to the prophetic authors, there are several key writers you should know. They are listed in the preceding chart. These men produced the majority of Scripture—how amazing to be filled so deeply with the Holy Spirit!

HOW THE STORY DEVELOPS

In a traditional Old Testament course, you learn the whole history of Israel and where you are in the story as you read along. This helps you make sense of what's going on and the messages God is trying to get across.

But, as stated in the last chapter, it's hard to get the big picture of what's going on in the Old Testament because it is not in chronological order—it is arranged by genre. First come the Law books, then the History books, then Wisdom books, then Major Prophets, and Minor Prophets. There is chronological order within each section, but it is difficult to make heads or tails of the entire Old Testament storyline because sections and books overlap.

For example, 2 Samuel and 1 Chronicles repeat stories because the same timeframe is covered by two different authors, Samuel and Ezra. Portions of Exodus and Deuteronomy also repeat because Moses reviews the Law twice with Israel. Books like 2 Chronicles and Psalms cover very large expanses of time—hundreds of years, which may not be evident at first.

Yet it's worth taking some time to figure out the whole story because where you are in God's redemptive history will guide your interpretation of the Biblical text.

God's revelation of Himself is progressive from Genesis to Revelation. Seeds that He planted early in the stories of Genesis come to full fruition by Revelation. In the middle, God builds His story of redemption and weaves themes in and out of the Biblical books. Perhaps you have heard of this idea in "the scarlet thread" of Jesus' blood being woven through the Old Testament. The same can be said of many things God wants us to understand, like healing and the Kingdom of God. These concepts grow throughout the Bible as the stories build upon each other.

Because God does this—builds revelation progressively—knowing where you are in the whole story is important. You can't figure out what the Old Testament means, derive theology from it, or apply it to your life correctly until you know the context of the story, character, or ritual.

To clarify, imagine for a moment that the Bible was a different story—like an Aesop's fable. Would you form the moral of the fable before the story was over? Such as while the hare was ahead of the tortoise? Of course not, because you would get a different moral!

In any piece of literature, you have to get to the end of the story to get the correct moral or perspective. Then you can read that backwards into the story. You can think back over the course of events you read earlier and understand how to interpret what was going on. Different details will stand out or take on deeper meaning as you do this. It's common to notice this when you reread a book you love or watch a movie a second time. You experience it much differently than when you went through it the first time.

The Bible is no different. God gave you an entire redemptive history in the Bible for this purpose. You examine the Bible as a whole story and make sure you know what's going on before you do anything else.

THE STORY IN MINIATURE

Now that you have some insight into the structure of the Bible, it's time to dive into an overview of the Bible's contents. Having a basic grasp of the flow of events will help you as you navigate through the complexities of the Bible story. We will go through these more slowly and carefully in the next several chapters.

The Beginning. The Bible opens with the book of Genesis, which provides the backdrop of Creation and what went wrong, as well as the first generations' experience of God's redemptive mission. After Adam and Eve fall, civilization decays and ends with God destroying violence and evil with the Flood.

Abraham and Moses. Afterwards, God reveals Himself to a man of faith, Abraham, who asserts his willingness to take the next step with Him. God hopes to extend this man's heart by creating an entire people group out of him—the Israelites—who will continue to walk with God and extend His goodness over the earth.

Moses is God's leader to spearhead the nation of Israel, where God attempts to dwell through the priesthood and contractual agreements, called covenants.

The History of Israel. Unfortunately, much of the Old Testament chronicles the failure of Israel to abide by these covenants, and God's repeated warnings to them that they need to repent and follow Him. The consequences for Israel was the loss of God dwelling with them and subsequent conquest by their enemies.

By the end of the Old Testament, the leadership of Israel has gone astray due to lack of faith, and the nation is poised to geographically disappear. The last book, Malachi, ends at the step in God's plan where God is ready to transfer the redemptive mission from Israel to the whole world.

The New Testament. The New Testament opens with a remnant of Jews still wanting to believe and follow God, even while under wayward leadership. They form the first people who, from the heart, want to seek Him.

Jesus is born within this nursery of faith and eventually calls twelve disciples to bring the news of forgiveness and reconciliation to Israel. He proclaims victory over evil, does many miracles to show who He is, and dies a sacrificial death to take away sin with its curses, once and for all. On the Cross, He took authority over Satan, the author of sin and death, and restored mankind to Adam's original place with God as an eternally loved child.

Jesus then rose from the dead, commissioned the gospel to go out to the world, and told all those who accepted Him to wait patiently for His return at the end of the age. The apostles after Him began to walk out this mission, and the New Testament closes with where they were in that quest, approximately 60 years later.

The story of the Old and New Testaments leads straight to you. The Church Age now continues where Biblical history ended. The history of the Church is full of how God's love and power has changed people and nations across the world. It has not been flawless, but has prevailed as the vessel of God's redemptive action on earth.

If you have accepted Jesus personally, you are now part of that legacy! Jesus is the Bible's unique solution to the problem of sin. Through Him, God himself entered history as a man to complete the redemption we needed. During His life, Jesus satisfied all the requirements Israel was not able to complete. He acted righteously in mankind's place and fulfilled all the rules and commandments the Law demanded. He also showed the true heart of God, that people made in His image should be able to live, have freedom, and experience love.

Ultimately, Christianity is an **evangelical** faith – the story of a people loved by God, inviting others into that same love. God continues to invite all men everywhere into a relationship with Him and asks those who accept Him to invite others. Anyone who accepts His sacrifice by faith and desires to be an extension of Jesus is saved from the destruction of Satan and evil at the end of time. They receive eternal life for the future but also a relationship with God while on earth. They walk in unity with their Father and His mission to save the world from its fallenness.

The great hope of the God of the Bible is that Scripture will help people make sense of this mission and accept it. The reason why we love and study the Word is to meet the One who wrote it, and be inspired to increase His Kingdom on earth the way He always hoped it would.

Chapter 5:
Old Testament Overview

Did you ever open the Old Testament and wonder what real story is it telling? Did you ever wish there was a timeline or cheat sheet to help you through it? It can be complicated to figure out what you're reading, especially with all the Hebrew names and ancient customs involved. The next two chapters will attempt to outline the most important events.

Part I: (Creation to 931BC*)

1. Creation
2. Adam and Eve
3. The Flood
4. The Tower of Babel
5. The Call of Abraham
6. Moses and the Exodus
7. Wandering in the Wilderness
8. Conquering the Promised Land
9. The Period of the Judges
10. The United Monarchy

Please note that dates until King David are approximate and generally taken from Jewish tradition.

CREATION

The very first period of history the Bible covers is **Creation**, in Genesis 1-2. We don't know the specifics of how and when the original event occurred, but Moses spoke by revelation that God made the heavens and earth **ex nihilo** (out of nothing) by speaking the Word. Biblical genealogies, including the one from Adam to

Christ (Luke 3:23-38), suggest this was approximately 6000-7000 years ago.

Other places in the Bible add to the meaning of Creation. John 1 says that all things were made by the Father for the Son. Creation is the foundation of Jesus' Lordship because the Father made all things by Him, through Him, and for Him.

The Psalms add that the earth is a footstool for His feet, and shows God's glory in visible form. It is also subject to His desires and intervention. The Prophets echo these ideas, as does the Book of Revelation which shows all things bending to God's will and coming into conformity with His ultimate purpose: to walk with mankind again in paradise.

ADAM AND EVE

Creation history spotlights the creation of man and woman, and how they were made to be in eternal relationship with God but lost this position because of sin.

Genesis 1-3 describes how God made man in His own image, the *imago Dei*. He made them male and female, and created them good. He blessed **Adam** by giving him **Eve**, his wife, and by giving him dominion over the created world.

God originally created mankind to never die. They were to spread His glory over the earth by walking in continual fellowship with Him. The vision was that each generation with their children, and all generations to come, would be a worldwide family who did great things while connected to the Lord. Then the whole earth would praise Him and give Him glory.

Adam and Eve, for a short time, tasted unbroken fellowship with the Lord. But they broke the first commandment to have no other gods before Him when they were tricked by the serpent, Satan. They listened to him, believed him, and therefore exchanged with Satan their own authority over creation (under God). This is traditionally called *"the Fall."* Sin entered the entire created order, and death—Satan's authored work—came with it, as sin's price.

God had to turn Adam and Eve out of paradise with the effects of sin all around them. He made a redemptive promise to them, though, that one day a Messiah would come from their own lineage and undo the curse of death by judging it. This was the beginning and end of the first phase of redemptive history.

THE FLOOD

Genesis 6-11 contains the next phase of redemptive history, between the time of Adam and Abraham.

Like the chapters which precede it, these provide just a sketch of what happened to God's first people. Adam and Eve are driven out of Eden, and sin begins to deepen and spread across the world immediately. Their first son, *Cain*, kills their second son, *Abel*, and the Lord provides a substitute son, *Seth*. From Seth will eventually come Noah, the only righteous man in his generation.

Cain's descendants become city-dwellers and the first enemies of the Lord. They are an advanced people with great engineering and artistic skills, but they fill the world with violence to such an extent that God is grieved He made man at all.

God then calls **Noah**, a priest of his generation, to build an ark and rescue himself, his family, and the animals of the earth from complete destruction. The plan is successful, and the world starts over with Noah and his three sons, Shem, Japheth, and Ham. Scripture calls this worldwide *Flood* a kind of "baptism" that prepares the world to start over, like believers do after they are born again and baptized (1 Peter 3:20-22).

From Noah's three sons come all the families of the world down to the present day. From Shem come the Semites (Jews and Arabs), from Japheth come the Indo-Europeans, and from Ham come the Canaanites. But Ham's descendants are cursed for Ham's disrespect towards his father. They become new enemies of the Lord who will eventually oppose the Jews.

THE TOWER OF BABEL

Before Noah's descendants fill the whole earth again, however, they congregate in *Babel.* They decide to build a tower to make a name for themselves and avoid dispersing as the Lord commanded them.

This is an evil plan. The leaders unite in pride against God and imply they will seize heaven back from Him—a sentiment that Satan himself articulates (Isaiah 14:13-14). Tradition holds that Nimrod was the architect of the tower, which was in Babylonian territory and therefore most likely a ziggurat-shaped temple.

Replica of a Babylonian Ziggurat

Since they are disobeying the command the Lord gave Noah, and Adam before him, to fill the whole earth and glorify God, God forcibly disperses them. He confuses their language so that they will break permanently into different groups and migrate away from Mesopotamia.

The Canaanites head south and west towards Israel and Africa, the Japhethites head north towards Assyria and Europe, and the Shemites spread throughout the Middle East. Having united in hate against God, the different people groups of the world are cursed to be fragmented so they can never fill the world with violence and cruelty again as they did in the days before Noah. Their lifespan is also shortened so that evil cannot proliferate to such an extent.

The Bible lists these earliest people groups on the renewed earth in Genesis 10 and calls it the **Table of Nations**. Tradition holds that there were about 70 original groups, which makes the number 70 a type of fullness in the rest of Scripture.

As the forerunners of each nation disperses, and ancestors pass down what they know, certain pieces of the true knowledge of God are lost. Different tribes retain different versions of the stories of Adam and Eve, sin, sacrifice, the Flood, their ancestors, and the Messiah to come. Ancient religions retain pieces of the truth but grow darker in their understanding as time goes on. Romans 1 describes how the will to follow God recedes, and so polytheism and idolatry take over the entire ancient world.

Also, as people divide into clans, the ancestral fathers take their different skills with them—some become city builders, some farmers, iron-workers, hunters, shipbuilders, etc. Civilization in Cain and Noah's days had comprehensive skills, but after Babel, general knowledge is fragmented by geography, language, and the shortened lifespan. Ancient civilizations therefore grow up with different specialties and abilities (or lack of them).

In recorded history, **Egypt** and **Babylon** (Sumer) are considered to be the earliest civilizations with geographic centers and advanced skills. Origins are sketchy but indicate somewhere between 4000-3000BC. Other civilizations in Peru and China may have started in that timeframe as well, as some ancient ruins indicate.

THE CALL OF ABRAHAM (CA. 2000BC)

Genesis 1-11 provides a quick gloss of history to provide a context for **Abraham**, the person with whom God really starts His redemptive action. In Genesis 12, history suddenly slows down. God telescopes in to describe one man who was full of faith enough to believe God and do incredible things—a spiritual father for all of us to follow.

Somewhere around 2000BC in the middle of ancient Sumer, God calls Abraham (then, "Abram") and asks him to leave the land of his fathers, Ur of Babylon. He asks him to separate from the world and pursue the true, living God. Abraham obeys and sets out for a place God says He will show him.

Along the way, Abraham receives the incredible promise that he will have a son and offspring as many as the stars. In this promise, God also says a nation will come out of him which will bless the entire world. By this, God means He intends to intervene and reassert the true knowledge of Him—that leads to renewed relationship with Him—back into the pagan world.

God gives Abraham wealth and everything he needs to make this happen, including the promise that his descendants will possess the land of Canaan (Israel). Even when Abraham makes mistakes in Egypt and with his own relatives, God forgives him, prospers him, and reminds him of His promises. God also uses Abraham to rescue his nephew Lot from Sodom and Gomorrah, where it has become clear how dark the darkness really is, and how Judgment will look when it finally comes.

When Abraham is 99 years old, God suddenly changes his name, circumcises him, and makes Sarah miraculously pregnant with a son, *Isaac*. When Isaac is a young boy, Abraham shows his superior commitment to God and belief in the resurrection to come by being willing to sacrifice his only beloved son on Mount Moriah. Seeing his willingness, God suspends the sacrifice by providing a ram in the bush. Abraham becomes the father of faith for all who will believe and follow God after him.

Subsequently, the history of the three patriarchs (fathers of faith), Abraham, Isaac, and Jacob, continues with many stories which are *typological,* or patterns to come. These include the first son rejecting the birthright and the second son choosing a better path; also the difficulty with Egypt and their Pharaoh, symbolizing the kingdoms of this world and the people who oppose God. These stories imbed and begin to grow through the remaining chapters of Genesis. Many prefigure certain aspects of Jesus, either who He is or what He will do.

The patriarchs live to be very old and have sons whom they hope will follow God. **Jacob** has twelve sons, one of whom is **Joseph**, who is sold into slavery in Egypt but rises to become second-in-command. Joseph saves everyone from famine, but the Hebrews' difficulty with Egypt heightens after he dies. The Kingdom of God eventually becomes enslaved by the Kingdom of Man.

This sets the stage for 400 years of bondage under Egypt, and the great cry for a deliverer who will rescue them.

MOSES AND THE EXODUS (CA. 1500BC)

The Book of Exodus opens with the Hebrews crying out to God. They have grown mighty in number, and a Pharaoh who knows nothing about their ancestry feels threatened by their presence in his nation. He enslaves them, oppresses them, and starts a campaign to kill their baby boys so they will not become stronger. Prefiguring the campaign to kill Jesus 1500 years later, the Pharaoh is a type of Antichrist.

Moses miraculously survives this threat at his birth. God guides him through 40 years in Egypt, and then 40 years more in the wilderness, to become Israel's deliverer. A murderer, shepherd, and stammerer, Moses is an unexpected candidate to lead a revolution. But after personally encountering God at the burning bush, he becomes strong enough in the Lord to confront Pharaoh.

With great displays of power, Moses tries to convince him to release God's people. Pharaoh famously refuses to let them go, and God sends ten plagues which devastate the Egyptian empire.

When the Hebrews escape the last one—the death of the firstborn, through sacrificial blood posted over their households—Pharaoh relents long enough for the Hebrews to pass on dry ground across the Red Sea with their cattle and the riches of Egypt. Pharaoh attempts to recapture them, but his army is drowned when the sea comes crashing back down. His empire's economy, military, society, and religion are now destroyed.

This is the first major incident of God starving the gods of the nations who rage against him. There will be others to come. Egypt shows everyone early on that salvation occurs through judgment, from which will escape only those who singularly believe by faith in God's power and sacrificial blood.

WANDERING IN THE WILDERNESS (CA. 1400BC)

The Israelites struggle in the Sinai desert after fleeing Egypt. God is trying to lead them to the Promised Land, a land flowing with milk and honey. He leads them by fire and cloud, heals them, and provides for all their needs. He even feeds them with bread from heaven. But His chosen people complain about everything and want to go back.

The end result of this is that they wander in a circle around the Sinai desert for 40 years. The entire journey was only supposed to take 11 days, but God causes them to wander until an entire generation who longed for Egypt, dies out. Moses himself is provoked to anger on several occasions but intercedes for his people by holding up the symbol of death's defeat—the serpent on the staff.

God is with Moses mightily and makes a new covenant that officially inaugurates the nation of Israel. At Mount Sinai, Moses spends 40 days personally receiving revelation from the Lord. He receives all the priestly and civil laws for Israel to become a nation which follows God.

Unfortunately, when Moses comes down with the first rules, the **Ten Commandments,** the people have already broken some of them by making a golden calf and worshipping the gods of Egypt. Moses breaks the first tablets in anger, and God makes a second set. This follows the typology of a second creation and a second law, written by the finger of God Himself.

Moses writes down the governmental and priestly laws of Israel in codified form so God's people will have it for perpetuity. These are the first five books of the Old Testament which are referred to as simply "the Law," or sometimes "the Law of Moses." They include blueprints and strict instructions on how to build a place for God to dwell—a tent of meeting called the *Tabernacle*.

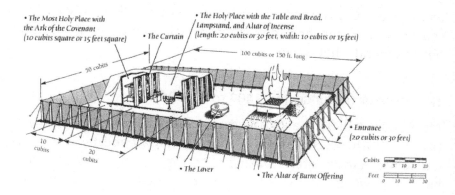

It also includes the rules for a priesthood so sacrifices can be made properly to atone for sin and sustain fellowship with a holy God. Everyone promises to obey these laws. They confirm this covenant with God with blood on the altar.

THE CONQUEST OF THE PROMISED LAND (CA. 1370BC)

In the end, Moses is only allowed to view the Promised Land from afar; he never enters. He dies at a very old age and his disciple, *Joshua*, is tapped to lead Israel into it.

It's a tough assignment to conquer Canaan, the Promised Land, but God shows Joshua and the people that He is with them as He was with Moses. God divides the waters of the Jordan River just as He did at the Red Sea. Joshua and his spies enter Jericho and are protected there by Rahab, who understands the signs of the times. The Israelite army then miraculously conquers Jericho.

Joshua leads multiple successful military campaigns to establish a base in the Promised Land, which leads to 31 separate kings being defeated there. Then God instructs Joshua to divide the land among the twelve tribes of Israel, fulfilling the covenant promise He originally made to Abraham that he would be given a land for his offspring to become a mighty nation.

As the people disperse and settle, Joshua reviews the history, the Law, and the Mosaic covenant with them (Joshua 24). He exhorts all Israel to obey the Lord. They promise they will. All is well for a season until Joshua and the high priest die, and a new generation has to defend what was won.

THE PERIOD OF THE JUDGES (CA. 1400 TO 1000BC)

After Joshua dies, the foothold gained by him and his army is tested. With no clear leader, Israel is threatened by war. The Canaanite religion starts mixing with their own. Israel becomes internally weak and is subsequently defeated and plundered (Judges 1-2).

The Lord then raises up *Judges*, different local leaders who govern Israel and save them from invaders. There are over a dozen Judges who defend Israel for 400 years. Gideon's army defeats the Midianites and Amalekites. Samson defeats the Philistine army, although tragically. Deborah is instrumental in delivering two of Israel's tribes from Canaanite oppression. The Book of Ruth is also written during this time.

While each Judge was alive, Israel would remain faithful to the Lord. But when the Judge died, the people would return to their idolatry, especially Baal worship which was customary in Canaanite religion. Their breaking the Lord's covenant permitted Israel's enemies to conquer them again and again.

A cycle of obedience and disobedience runs its course for approximately 400 years. This greatly disturbs the Lord, who had previously rescued His people from 400 years of slavery under Egypt.

At the end of the period of Judges, disobedience eventually results in civil war and anarchy where "everyone did what was right in their own eyes" (Judges 21:25). Israel's existence was in trouble.

THE UNITED MONARCHY (ABOUT 1051BC TO 931BC)

Samuel. God raises up **Samuel** as the last righteous Judge and a type of Christ—a prophet and priest, born through a miraculous birth and devoted to God from infancy. Samuel judges righteously but faces the problem of a continuously backsliding Israel, including a corrupt priesthood under Hophni and Phineas.

The Israelites bring the sign of their glory and covering, the Ark of the Covenant, onto the battlefield. They believe it will ensure them victory, but it does not. The Philistines capture the Ark, and the glory departs from Israel.

Replica of the Ark of the Covenant

King Saul. Refusing to believe that their defeat has anything to do with their hearts toward God, Israel demands a king against God's warning (1 Samuel 8). Samuel anoints their first king, **Saul**, who initially seems impressive.

But eventually Saul brings Israel down. He performs the holy sacrifices himself (instead of letting the priest do it), and spares the king of the Amalekites against God's command. He also keeps their spoils of war, worldly treasures. Saul has disgraced his reign. At

God's prompting, Samuel anoints the next king, the youthful shepherd David.

King David. From external appearances, *David* is another unlikely candidate for the Lord's favor. But he proves himself a man of faith when he defeats Goliath. This puts the Philistines on notice that the Lord may be reprising.

David rises in the ranks of King Saul's army until Saul begins to hunt him down, chasing him through caves. God protects David until Saul dies. Then the tribe of Judah makes David their king (ca. 1011-971BC).

After Saul's son and general are killed, and there is no one left to vie for the throne, David's first battle as king is to conquer Jerusalem. He makes this his capital and has huge military success, restoring security to Israel as a nation. Over time, David becomes the king of all Israel, uniting the twelve tribes at age 30—the same age that Jesus began His ministry.

Additionally, David returns true worship to Israel. He recaptures the Ark of the Covenant and restores a pure priesthood. He expresses his joy and trust in God's protection through the Psalms, which are largely written during his reign. He is a man after God's own heart, so even when he falls into sin with Bathsheba, God forgives him and prospers Israel.

David's willingness to act and repent is one of the best examples for us in the Bible. His inner thoughts are given to us in the Psalms, which reveal a startlingly personal and loving relationship with God. As a result, God makes a covenant with David and promises him an eternal dynasty. He promises that he will always have a king on the throne of Israel, and the Messiah will come from his lineage.

King Solomon. After David dies, there is a brief time of unparalleled prosperity and unity for Israel. David's son **Solomon** succeeds him as king (ca. 971-931BC). Solomon's first years are known as the Golden Age of Israel because of the wealth and peace that characterize them.

Replica of Solomon's Temple

After praying for the gift of wisdom, Solomon builds the **Temple** for God to dwell in and transfers the Ark into it. He creates an empire of splendor unmatched in the ancient world—so brilliant that the Queen of Sheba bows down to him, and gold pours into the kingdom. Trade is established all over the Middle East, and hundreds of concubines come in as homage and payment from neighboring lands.

The End of an Era. Unfortunately, the enormous harem that Solomon amasses draws him away from God. Although he is the wisest man of his time, he makes a very unwise choice to permit foreign women who worship strange gods into his sphere. They mix worship of the true God with worship of the pagan gods around Israel, causing the same problem which brought Israel down during the period of the Judges.

Israel's brilliant monarchy therefore ends on a sad note. The same man who wrote the stunning wisdom of the Proverbs, and prophesied the divine romance of Jesus and the Church in the Song of Solomon, ends his life with the sad, existential writings of Ecclesiastes.

Solomon's sin leads not only to his personal downfall, but to the division of his kingdom (1 Kings 11). The breaking of the Lord's commandments breaks the Golden Age of the strongest empire in history.

Chapter 6:
Old Testament: Kingdom Divided

The first half of the history of Israel signals how the second half will go. The rest of the Old Testament is a story of how God's redemptive purposes are not held in the hearts of His people enough to preserve them for His ultimate purpose—to deliver mankind from sin and the power of the devil.

Instead, God's people waver and spend the next 500 years trying to escape the slide into corruption and extinction. The prophets are the main tools the Lord uses to turn the hearts of kings and people back to Him, but they have limited effectiveness. The Old Testament ends with Israel as a nation being sent into captivity and overcome by their enemies.

Part II:
1. The Kingdom Divides
2. The Prophets' Ministry
3. Judah Fends for Itself
4. Exile to Babylon
5. Return from Exile
6. Intertestamental Period

THE KINGDOM DIVIDES (CA. 931-722BC)

All twelve tribes of Israel were united under the reigns of Saul, David, and Solomon. When King Solomon dies, however, his son **Rehoboam** takes the throne. The Israelites are exhausted from Solomon's rule and the elders counsel Rehoboam to be more lenient with them. Instead, Rehoboam is harsh. This leads to a rebellion led by **Jeroboam**, an Israelite who had been exiled in Egypt.

At the end of their civil conflict, Israel is broken into two kingdoms, never to reunite. Rehoboam, Solomon's son, retains the kingship of the tribes of Judah and Benjamin in the south. This is called "*Judah*" in the Biblical text from that point on, or sometimes "*Jerusalem*" after its capital.

Jeroboam becomes king of the ten tribes in the north. This is called "*Israel*" in the text from that point on, or "*Samaria*" after its capital. Both the kingdoms of Judah and of Israel have a long list of kings that govern their region.

The chart on the next page summarizes the kings of the northern kingdom of Israel. Even though northern Israel is bigger, wealthier, and more powerful than Judah, it falls first to foreign captors. The books of 1 and 2 Kings and 1 and 2 Chronicles document how all of north Israel's kings were unfaithful to the Lord. They set up high places and adopted all the practices of the nations that the Lord had previously driven out.

The kings of Israel also ignored and persecuted the prophets whom God sent to warn them. Since the civil government was such a powerful entity, God used prophets outside the mainstream to confront the kings' evil and exhort them to turn back to the pure worship of the Lord. Some also preached to Jewish crowds or leadership.

Kings of Israel (Northern Kingdom)			
King	Begin	Years	Reference
Jeroboam I	931 BC	22 years	1 Ki 12:25-14:20
Nadab	910 BC	2 years	1 Ki 15:25-32
Baasha	909 BC	24 years	1 Ki 15:33-16:7
Elah	886 BC	2 years	1 Ki 16:8-14
Zimri	885 BC	7 days	1 Ki 16:15-20
Omri	885 BC	12 years	1 Ki 16:21-28
Ahab	874 BC	22 years	1 Ki 17-22:40
Ahaziah	853 BC	2 years	1 Ki 22:51- 2 Ki 1:16
Joram	852 BC	12 years	2 Ki 1:17-8:15
Jehu	841 BC	28 years	2 Ki 9-10

Jehoahaz	814 BC	17 years	2 Ki 13:1-9
Jehoash	798 BC	16 years	2 Ki 13:10-14:20
Jeroboam II	782 BC	41 years	2 Ki 14:25-29
Zechariah	753 BC	6 mo	2 Ki 15:8-12
Shallum	752 BC	1 mo	2 Ki 15:13-16
Menahem	752 BC	10 years	2 Ki 15:17-22
Pekahiah	742 BC	2 years	2 Ki 15:23-26
Pekah	740 BC	20 years	2 Ki 15:27-31
Hoshea	732 BC	9 years	2 Ki 17

Many kings, like Ahab, had no moral compass at all. Most of them expanded the worship of Baal and Asherah (Baal's mother and mistress). These were extremely crude, pagan cults rivaling the true worship of the Lord. They institutionalized bloodletting, child sacrifice, worshipping phallic gods and totems, incest, and prostitution with the priesthood.

The next chart lists some of the main prophets to northern Israel: Elijah and Elisha are among the first to battle Baal worship in northern Israel. Later on, Amos, Isaiah, and Hosea bring words of condemnation as things grow worse. But they are unable to turn the tide. There are no revivals or godly kings in northern Israel.

Northern Prophets—Israel, 1050-722BC			
Prophet	**Date**	**Prophesied To**	**Prophesied About**
Samuel	1050-1000BC	Israel/Judah	King Saul's conduct, David's rightful place
Nathan	ca. 1000BC	Israel/Judah	King David's conduct
Elijah	875-849BC	Israel	Israel's idolatry
Elisha	848-797BC	Israel	Israel's idolatry
Jonah	770BC	Assyria	Ninevah must repent
Amos	760BC	Israel	Judgment on Israel
Hosea	760-730BC	Israel	Israel's captivity coming
Isaiah	740-700BC	Israel/Judah	Judgment on Israel and its oppressors

Many Old Testament laws were set up in opposition to the laws of Baal, and much of the imagery the Hebrew prophets used came from what the Israelites were doing against the Lord as they worshipped the wrong gods.

Eventually, the Assyrians—a warrior civilization whose cruelty has been historically compared to the Nazis—sack the northern kingdom in 722BC. They destroy Samaria, the government seat. The Israelites are taken into captivity, and the prophecies of Micah document this sad moment.

THE PROPHETS' MINISTRY

Let us pause for a moment to consider the Prophetic writings, which overlap Old Testament history. When studying the Prophets, there are a few helpful things to know.

First, there were many Hebrew prophets who did not author a book of the Bible. Elijah, Elisha, Micaiah, Iddo, and others do not have their own books.

Secondly, there were many prophets, not just the famous ones. The prophetic office was an important arm of the Lord's ministry. Scripture tells us there were "schools of prophets" under Samuel, Elijah, and Elisha, where many were being trained. We also know from 1 Kings 18 that at least 100 prophets were saved from Jezebel. Similarly, in Jonah's story, the Lord tells him there were 7000 who had not bowed their knee to Baal.

Prophets were important in the history of Israel because they brought revival, miracles, and truth to a civilization that was constantly going astray. They often opposed "court prophets" who told the Israelite kings what they wanted to hear. The Lord used his real prophets mightily, but only a small percentage of them became authors of Scripture, possibly because only some had the education to be able to do so.

Major and Minor Prophets. In the Bible, there are sixteen prophets who wrote books of Scripture. Four are classified as "Major Prophets" and twelve are classified as "Minor Prophets," as follows:

The division of prophets into these two categories is somewhat misleading because the terms "Major Prophet" and "Minor Prophet" refer to *how long* a book the prophet authored, not how *important* they were. Isaiah is a "Major Prophet" because his book is 66 chapters long—not because he was more important than Zechariah, who wrote a shorter book, or Elijah, who wrote no book at all.

While the Major Prophets are listed in chronological order, and the Minor Prophets mostly are also, many prophets' lifespans overlap each other. For example, Isaiah overlaps with Hosea and Micah, and Jeremiah overlaps with Zephaniah and Daniel. It can take quite a bit of work to figure out how everyone's timeline interrelates.

Major Prophets	Minor Prophets
Isaiah	Hosea
Jeremiah	Joel
Ezekiel	Amos
Daniel	Obadiah
	Jonah
	Micah
	Nahum
	Habakkuk
	Zephaniah
	Haggai
	Zechariah
	Malachi

Also complicating the Prophets is the fact that some books like Isaiah's contain prophetic messages spoken over a long time period, while others like Jonah's and Obadiah's are momentary "snapshots." And although all the prophetic books are located at the end of your Old Testament, their lifetimes overlap the stories from the History section. Nahum's ministry, for example, fits into the last third of 2 Chronicles. Nehemiah fits in between Ezra 8 and 9. Since there are various authorship theories in academic circles, there are quite a variety of online charts that attempt to diagram how the prophets "plug back" into the history correctly.

Lastly, neither the order nor the designation "Major" or "Minor" Prophet indicates where the prophet was prophesying to. Some prophesied to the northern kingdom of Israel, the southern kingdom of Judah, or both. Some prophesied to enemy kingdoms like Assyria. Many prophesied to more than one group, or moved locations during their lifetime. Ezekiel, for example, started off in Judah prophesying about their captivity, but ended up in Babylon prophesying about Judah's return and restoration.

First Wave	Second Wave	Third Wave
Amos	Micah*	Haggai
Hosea	Obadiah*	Joel**
Jonah	Nahum	Zechariah
Isaiah	Habakkuk	Malachi
	Zephaniah	
	Jeremiah	
	Ezekiel	
	Daniel	
	*crossover figure	**debated

The most helpful way to understand the Prophets is to divide them into "three waves": those who spoke primarily about events pertinent to the northern kingdom of Israel, those who spoke primarily to the southern kingdom of Judah before or during their exile, and those who spoke after the exile about the days coming to the faithful.

The main thing you need to know about prophets is that they were all sent to keep God's chosen people on the straight and narrow path. Most pronounced judgment on Israel, most pronounced even harsher judgment on their enemies, and many prophesied about zeal and glory to come, including the Messiah and End Times events.

JUDAH FENDS FOR ITSELF (722-596BC)

After the northern kingdom of Israel falls to Assyria in 722BC, the southern kingdom of Judah is left standing for another 150 years. It is a smaller kingdom but has several good kings: Asa, Jehoshaphat, Uzziah, Jotham, Hezekiah, and Josiah. Also aiding their protection is the Ark of the Covenant, which Judah held in the Temple at Jerusalem.

The following is a list of the kings of Judah, from 930-530BC:

Kings of Judah				
King	**Good/Bad**	**Began**	**Years**	**Reference**
Rehoboam	Bad	930 BC	17	1 Ki 11:42-14:31
Abijah	Bad	913 BC	3	1 Ki 14:31-15:8
Asa	Good	911 BC	41	1 Ki 15:8-24
Jehoshaphat	Good	870 BC	25	1 Ki 15:24, 22:41-51
Jehoram	Bad	848 BC	8	2 Ki 8:16-24
Ahaziah	Bad	841 BC	1	2 Ki 8:24-29, 9:14-26
Athaliah	Bad	841 BC	6	2 Ki 8:26, 11:1-20
Joash	Good	835 BC	40	2 Ki 11:1-12:21
Amaziah	Good	796 BC	29	2 Ki 14:1-22
Uzziah	Good	781 BC	52	2 Ki 15:1-7
Jotham	Good	740 BC	16	2 Ki 15:32-38
Ahaz	Bad	736 BC	16	2 Ki 15:38-16:20
Hezekiah	Good	716 BC	29	2 Ki 18:1- 20:21
Manasseh	Bad	697 BC	55	2 Ki 21:1-18
Amon	Bad	642 BC	2	2 Ki 21:18-26
Josiah	Good	640 BC	31	2 Ki 21:26-23:30
Jehoahaz	Bad	609 BC	<1	2 Ki 23:30-34
Jehoiakim	Bad	609 BC	11	2 Ki 23:34-24:6
Jehoiachin	Bad	598 BC	<1	2 Ki 24:6-17
Zedekiah	Bad	597 BC	11	2 Ki 24:17-25:30

Judah's track record is very bumpy, and many kings follow in the way of their counterparts in the north, permitting false religions to grow and adulterate the pure worship of the Lord. Multiple prophets are sent from God, who tries to motivate them to return to Him.

Southern Prophets—Judah, 722BC-520BC			
Prophet	Date	To	Prophesied About
Isaiah	740-700BC	Israel/ Judah	Warning that what happened to Israel would happen to Judah
Micah	737-690BC	Judah	Fall of Israel and Judah
Nahum	650BC	Assyria	Judgment on Ninevah
Habakkuk	630BC	Judah	The Coming Babylonians
Zephaniah	627BC	Judah	Days of Wrath coming
Jeremiah	627-580BC	Judah	Babylonian Captivity impending
Ezekiel	593-570BC	Jews in Babylon	The Fall of Jerusalem
Daniel	605-530BC	Babylon	World Empires to come

Under the prophets' influence, Judah experiences four major religious revivals. In those times, the peoples' recommitment to the true and living God keeps their enemies from conquering them. The entire time, Judah is surrounded by major global powers including Assyria, Egypt, Babylon, and the Ammonites, Moabites, and Arameans. Small but mighty, Judah is able to shine the light in several important moments.

Josiah is the last good king Judah has. After he dies and his religious reforms are not upheld, it is inevitable that Judah will be swallowed up by one of their neighbors—it is simply a question of who and when.

EXILE TO BABYLON (606-538BC)

Between about 650-600BC, The Kingdom of Judah receives warnings from Nahum, Zephaniah, and Habbakuk that conquest is coming and it is going to be the end of Judah. When captivity finally comes, it happens in three waves:

Three Waves of Exile			
Date	Event	Scripture	Taken
606 BC	Judah conquered.	Jer. 25:1	Daniel
597 BC	Nebuchadnezzar punishes Jehoiakin.	Jer. 52:28 2 Ki 24:12	Ezekiel
586 BC	Nebuchadnezzar punishes Zedekiah. Jerusalem destroyed.	2 Ki 25:8	

As Jewish captives are exiled deeper into Babylonian territory, God continues to offer mercy and forgiveness to them if they will turn and repent. Yet they refuse. Each time they resist, the punishment becomes more severe. During the second wave of exile, many Jewish prisoners of war are killed and the Temple is taken.

In 586BC, Nebuchadnezzar completes the conquest. He destroys Jerusalem's walls and burns down the Temple, palaces, and houses. The last Israelite king, Zedekiah, flees but is captured and taken to Nebuchadnezzar. He is forced to watch as his sons get executed. Then his eyes are put out and he is led away in chains while the final deportation of Jews begin. It is a startling and symbolic end to the first incarnation of Israel, recorded in Jeremiah and 2 Kings.

Even in such despair, God offers glimmers of hope. The prophets, as they pronounce harsh judgment upon Israel and Judah for their sins, also prophesy the returning of the Lord's favor. The book of Isaiah, for example, has over twenty chapters which prophesy blessing to come upon the Lord's people. The Minor Prophets proclaim that once Israel's captors have taken her away, that judgment will come upon them for attacking the Lord's anointed and showing them no mercy. They echo Jesus' words that, "These things must come, but woe to them through whom they come!" (Luke 17:1).

The same theme runs through Jeremiah, who is the main chronicler of history in this period. He records the last five kings of Judah as well the fact that only a wide movement of repentance can save them. Weeping, he gives the last appeal to Judah, begging them to repent before Nebuchadnezzar attacks. Meanwhile, the king of Judah exhorts Jeremiah to pray for deliverance and report back to him that their nation will not be destroyed.

Jeremiah knows what is coming, however, and prophesies the duration of the Babylonian captivity—70 years. He never sees the end of it because he dies in Babylon before the exile is over. But like the other prophets before him, he foretells the judgment which will befall Israel's enemies and the future restoration of God's people.

Vassals of Babylon. Next to being enslaved in Egypt, Israel's exile in Babylon is one of the darkest periods in their history. The Jews are subsumed first in Babylonian, then Persian civilization. The Temple worship is gone and there is no cohesive element to their identity. Ezekiel is among the Jews deported to Babylon and prophesies much like Jeremiah, about how they got into all this trouble and when they will eventually get out—i.e. when their dry bones will grow new skin.

During this time, the era of history begins that some scholars call *the Axial Age.* It is when many of the world's greatest (non-Biblical) religious traditions begin, including Buddhism, Zoroastrianism, Jainism, and Taoism. In China, Confucianism comes the enshrined, orthodox belief system at this time. In Eastern Europe, Greek paganism with all their gods and goddesses becomes formalized. The Temple of Zeus is built, and the first signs of Greek ascendancy come into view, including the first great Greek philosophers (Socrates, Aristotle, and Plato).

All of these things happen while Israel is exiled. It is as if while the true Lord's presence is muzzled in the world, other gods' presences are unleashed.

Some experts have theorized that the *diaspora* of the Jews to the far corners of the world actually catalyzed this great religious shift by impacting the traditions wherever they went. While we may never know the exact spiritual connection, it is true that the end of the nation of Israel is historically connected with a major shift in almost every world religion that is organized at this time.

In the midst of this, you see in the accounts of Daniel and Esther that some Jews are able to retain their pure worship of God. They are frowned upon but tolerated in certain ways. Daniel is the respected counsel to a series of pagan kings during the exile, most notably Nebuchadnezzar who started all the trouble. The book of Daniel has the most exile history in it, talking about the values of Babylon and its transition to Persian rule.

Then Daniel prophesies the order and fate of the upcoming empires prior to the Messiah, as well as the exact timing of Christ and His authority over the earth (Daniel 7-9). Some Bible scholars think the magi came from Babylon, having been exposed to Daniel's prophecies.

Captivity Ends. Regardless, the Babylonian captivity officially ends in 538BC when the Decree of Cyrus allows Jews to return to Jerusalem. This gives Israel a chance to start over and fulfills the great prophecy of Isaiah 44-45 (from 150 years earlier!) that a great "shepherd" who did not "know the Lord" would "open doors" for God's people to return as a nation.

Return from Exile (538BC- ca. 400BC)

The Persians release any Jews who want to return home. Over the next century, waves of Jews start returning to Jerusalem. Just as there were three waves of prophets, and three waves of exile, there are also three distinct returns from Babylon:

Three Returns from Exile		
Date	**Event**	**Leader**
536 BC	Cyrus allows the Jews to return	Zerubbabel
458 BC	Ezra brings revival to the people	Ezra
445 BC	Nehemiah gets permission from Artaxerxes to rebuild the city.	Nehemiah

The first group of returning Jews are led by Zerubbabel, a descendent of King David. He initiates the rebuilding of the second Temple. Then the Persians support Ezra going home, and he becomes the main chronicler of post-exile history.

The second Temple is completed soon afterwards, in 515BC, by which time Haggai and Zechariah have been written. There is great hope that the Lord will dwell again in Israel. Faithful Jews believe that His Messiah will soon come and initiate the great sequence of judgment and blessing which the prophets foretold.

Thirty years later, the book of Esther records the events which almost exterminated the entire Jewish population still living in Persia. This motivates a second wave of immigrants to return to Israel with Ezra in 458BC.

Post-Exile Prophets Jerusalem 520BC-440BC			
Prophet	Date	Prophesied To	Prophesied About
Haggai	520BC	Judah	The Second Temple
Zechariah	520-518BC	Judah	Visions of the coming Lord
Joel	??	Judah	The Last Days
Ezra	457-448BC	Jerusalem	Returning from Babylon, rebuilding the Temple
Nehemiah	444BC	Jerusalem	Rebuilding Jerusalem
Malachi	443BC	Judah	The Messiah; judgment

A third wave comes with Nehemiah when he gets permission to rebuild the walls of Jerusalem. He encounters much resistance but gets the project done. Afterwards, Ezra re-reads the Law aloud in the city, and the people declare their willingness to start over with God (Ezra 10). Their hope is that this re-creation will work and Israel will witness the final salvation, deliverance, and judgment on sin that has been prophesied since the beginning. They will win and their enemies will be defeated!

Resettlement. Unfortunately, history is condemned to repeat itself without the Jews' clear understanding of why they were permitted to be destroyed in the first place. The last prophet, Malachi, prophesies to the new group of Jews in Jerusalem under Nehemiah's leadership when they go into idolatry again, around 435-410BC.

The Lord is compassionate in His warnings and ends the Old Testament with a promise of future restoration and redemption that He will one day turn "the hearts of the fathers to their children and the hearts of the children to their fathers" (4:16). It's a different kind of prophecy—one that seems to be opening a new era. It's a glimpse into the kind of radical heart change that is going to be Jesus' motive and message when He comes as that promised Deliverer.

At this point, a Jewish remnant is preserved because of God's faithfulness to Abraham, Moses, David, and those who followed Him. The faithful are waiting in hope for the Lord to return and restore a glorious kingdom to Israel through the hands of an anointed one, the Messiah. They are also believing for the Great Judgment which will punish the nations who persecuted them throughout history.

They do not know that 400 years are going to go by before deliverance comes—the same number of years as the Israelites were enslaved in Egypt before they were led out by their deliverer into the Promised Land. During this time, the Jews try but are not able to reconstruct the glory days of the past. God has moved on from the past and is preparing the world for the glory days to come—the "latter days" of the future (Isaiah 2:2).

INTERTESTAMENTAL PERIOD (CA. 420BC-0 AD)

After the Book of Malachi, the Old Testament canon closes and Biblical history stops. Secular history of course does not, and we jump into a *very* new world with John the Baptist 400 years later.

Suddenly the Roman Empire is dominant, with Caesar and a system of governors. The Jews are scorned but tolerated as long as they pay taxes to Rome. They speak Greek, go to synagogues, and obey new leaders like the Pharisees and Saduccees... What happened in the interim?

Out of Babylon. In Israel, the canonization of the Hebrew Bible begins during this time. The written Word as codified by the *Sanhedrin* (their legal and judicial authorities) becomes the new foundation for living under God. It begins to be commonly read during Jewish liturgy throughout the week.

This causes the Jewish population to develop varying interpretations of what has happened to them. Some interpret their exile in Babylon like their exile in Egypt—that the Lord is going to send a deliverer and begin their nation anew with glory.

Others insist that because Israel hadn't been unfairly taken into slavery, like they had been in Egypt, that a lack of glory was their due punishment for breaking their covenant and embracing idolatry.

Still others think their captivity was a prelude to the End of all of history—that God is done with them and therefore the world will soon be over. Each of these perspectives is reflected in some ways in the Prophets; these views were not mutually exclusive.

Fast forwarding a little, Jesus' disciples also reflect a mix of these views. They hoped that He, as Messiah, was going to restore the kingdom back to Israel. Yet it became clear as Jesus approached crucifixion that He was not going to do that, at least not in the way they expected. They then briefly considered that a lack of glory was their lot. At the end of the New Testament, in the Book of Revelation, the apostle John invoked "Babylon" as the ultimate enemy of God's people because of the historical association of "Babylon" as a type of "the End of all history," with the Lord destroying the worldly captors of His kingdom.

So the Jews coming out from Babylon form a new post-exile identity that the Jews of Jesus' day still have, and interpret those events by. This new identity takes into account everything they had been through, and everything that had been prophesied to them since the time of Abraham, based on Scriptural prophecy. Jesus essentially validates this identity but greatly changes their interpretation and application of it, as well as their interpretation of the Word.

Persian Rule. The Persians were the ones who inherited the Babylonian Empire and who initially gave the Jews permission to return to Jerusalem. Successive emperors let Jews return in waves until approximately 330BC, but many Jewish people did not go and remained in Persian territory. This is how Aramaic (the Persian language) became a common language for Jews, including for Daniel, Ezra, and Jesus, and why portions of the Old Testament text are in Aramaic.

This is also the age when the institution of the **synagogue** was formed to offer a "church" of sorts for those who could not regularly attend Sabbath services at the Temple in Jerusalem. Scripture was read publicly several times per week, and **Pharisees** became local guards of purity and correct doctrine at different locations, similar to pastors and teachers. This was in conjunction with the **Sadducees** who claimed priestly lineage and directed the rituals performed in the Temple at Jerusalem.

Greek Rule. Alexander the Great then conquered vast territory in the late fourth century BC, and when he did so, Greek language and customs spread everywhere he ruled, including Persia and Israel. Judaism came under Greek domination and many Jews were *Hellenized* or made Greek.

This is how the Hebrew Bible ended up being translated into Greek and called the **Septuagint**. This is also how *koine* Greek got to be the common language the New Testament authors would write in.

Observant Jews tried to resist Hellenization by keeping their rites and rituals going. This annoyed Roman authorities but were extremely important to the lawyers and teachers who led the Jewish people. They were seen as the guardians of the faith. Jesus will end up confronting some of the rituals and their motives behind them.

Egyptian Rule. For a brief period after Alexander the Great died, the Egyptians (Ptolemies) governed Israel. However, the Egyptians had also been Hellenized, so the Greek way of life did not change for the Jews.

Syrian Rule. The Syrians (Seleucids) battled Egypt for control of Jewish territory and won. They were also a Hellenized culture. This was an especially dark period of history for the Jews because the Syrian kings were extremely hostile to them practicing their faith. Antiochus Epiphanes, for example, whose name meant "God Manifest," massacred 120,000 Jews and burned sections of Jerusalem down. Then he outlawed Jewish observance and declared the Temple a temple of Zeus. He executed resistors and slaughtered unclean animals on the altar, defiling the building. This led directly to the Jewish revolt under the Maccabees in 166BC.

Jewish Revolt. In the Maccabean revolt, a Jewish priest Matthias and his sons defeated the Syrians in a series of battles. They won independence for Judah and founded their own dynasty (the Hasmoneans) which was dedicated to spreading Scriptural Judaism again.

The Maccabean Revolt

This is when the parties of Pharisees and Sadducees were formalized, with Sadducees comprised mainly of priestly and aristocratic classes, and Pharisees being the more populist party which emphasized Mosaic purity laws and rejected Greek customs. Also at this time, teachings concerning the Messiah began to proliferate and prepare the hearts of the Jewish people. They became hopeful that someone was going to come and deliver them out of pagan rule.

Roman Rule. The Jews were in control of Judah from 166- 63BC, when the Romans conquered most of the old Greek empire including Israel. The Romans majored on stabilizing their colonies, so they installed a friendly king, Herod, as king of Judah (renamed *Judea,* in Greek).

The Romans set up a rival authority system for the Jews, just as previous empires had, with laws and taxes which had to be honored by them. Their governing structure is most apparent in the events at the end of Jesus' life when He is tried before a series of Roman governors who, with the Jews' instigation, find Him guilty and crucify Him. It can also be seen in the major life events of Paul, who has dual citizenship with Israel and Rome but ends up on house arrest in Rome and ultimately martyred there.

While God was of course not done with His people, the Old Testament inspired Word did close for the 400 years between Malachi, the last prophet, and Jesus' birth. It is a different world that Jesus will be born into, yet He speaks to His people almost as if nothing has changed. He essentially calls them back to God in the same manner that the Old Testament prophets did—except this time under a new and different covenant that greatly tests their interpretation of life since leaving Babylon.

CONCLUSION

You don't have to be a history expert to apply God's Word, but God put a lot of history in the Bible for a reason! He could have skipped it all if it didn't matter.

Having an overview of Old Testament history makes it make a lot more sense. You know why the prophets are warning people that certain judgments are coming, and what those judgments were about. You know the blessings and character of God as well, and how the first kingdom of God was supposed to look.

The thing to keep in mind is that, despite the wars and kings and interruptions, the Old Testament is a love story. It is God the Father's record of reaching out to humanity over the years, and trying to prepare an entire people to walk with Him as He had intended with Adam in the Garden.

Chapter 7:
Themes in the Old Testament

Understanding the history behind the Old and New Testaments is a good starting point. But you can easily learn everything about Bible history and still miss the actual message of the Bible! They're not the same thing.

The message of the Bible is God's loving outreach—His redemption and restoration of us to Himself. After Adam and Eve fall, God sets out on a massive redemptive and restorative crusade to get mankind back. He carves out a people for Himself from nothing, gives them a code to live by that will put them in basic fellowship with Him. Then, through Jesus, God purchases us back. He pays the huge price of sin—from the first one to the very last. This opens an invitation to all who want to come into fellowship with God to do so before the end of history. We acknowledge that price and come under the shelter of our glorious Savior.

This final phase is where we are living. The Church stands as a lighthouse to the world until God decides the crusade is over. He will return to judge evil itself, and then redemption and restoration will be complete.

Themes in Genesis. The foundations of this redemptive and restoration mission are begun in the Book of Genesis. So is the struggle against sin and the corresponding war against God through that which is under the Fallen domain of the devil.

For this reason, it is important to pause and examine some foundational concepts in Genesis. Many of them are keys to interpreting the rest of the Bible. One famous Bible interpreter called Genesis the "seed plot" of the Bible for containing the "seed" things the Lord has planted and is expecting to harvest at the end of the age.

Through key events in Genesis, we see God's character and His plan. We see His perspective on the entire fallen situation. We see Him act with love, holiness, and zeal. We see how He prefers to act—the true ways redemption and restoration will work.

These are all things to look for as you read through each book in the Bible. You have to put on your "big picture" glasses. Themes which begin in Genesis in miniature progressively expand throughout the entire Bible... and even into history after the Bible! One day, it will all conclude with a massive victory for us and for God, and everything God has worked with us to accomplish will be complete. He will have back what He lost, and so will we.

IN THE BEGINNING: RELATIONSHIP

God has existed eternally in three Persons as the Father, Son, and Holy Spirit. It was out of this relationship that God created the universe and mankind. Importantly, Genesis 1 does not say, "Let me make man in my image," but rather, "Let *us* make man in *our* image."

This tells us that one of God's primary purposes in Creation was relationship. He created through relationship, and then brought us into that relationship, to co-create more.

When God created Adam and Eve, they were to multiply and fill the whole earth. God did not create an individual, or even multiple individuals, but a family—a husband and wife, whom He married and then told to have children. They reflected His relational nature.

Additionally, these children were never meant to die. As these children had children, and so forth, the entire earth would be filled with one large family. This family would relate to God for the rest of eternity with Him, bringing forth life, dominion, and blessing. That was God's original intent.

We see almost immediately, however, that although God called everything He created "good," there was something outside the Garden that was not good – a deceptive and evil serpent. Where did this serpent come from? Why don't we see God creating any such evil?

What we find out later is that this serpent was Satan, the greatest of the angels, who was created good but then fell and began a rebellion against God. (This story is told in various places including Job, Isaiah, Ezekiel, and Revelation.) Satan had already broken relationship with God. He knew he was sentenced to hell and wanted to take us—God's glory, His children—with him.

This alludes to a second purpose God had in creation – the permanent and final defeat of evil, personified by His enemy, Satan. When God placed man in the garden, He told him to "take dominion" over the fish and the birds, and "every living creature that moves on the ground" (Gen 1:28). It was not long until this serpent, moving on the ground, appeared.

In other words, God had in mind and knew from the beginning that there would be a conflict. He had placed man there to win it! Adam was to be like God's avatar in the battle, confronting and defeating Satan, a created being, inside the created universe.

As we know, Adam did not confront and defeat the serpent. Instead he was defeated and taken captive by the serpent. He therefore exchanged his godly nature for the same evil nature Satan had.

This was the Fall of man—the conversion of God's only player on the field to the enemy's team. And not only did God lose man, but since man was placed in the Garden as a ruler of creation, creation itself was lost too. In the words of John Milton, it was truly "paradise lost." In order to win against Satan, God planned to recapture His player and then use him to complete the mission. The Bible is the story of this quest.

The master themes of all of history are therefore God developing His family and His progressive defeat of evil. How can God not only regain everything He has lost, but also defeat the evil one who stole it from Him?

RESTORATION THROUGH COVENANT

God has chosen a special instrument for the process of restoration: the *covenant*. A covenant is an agreement or a treaty between two people, similar to a "contract" but with the goal of ushering in peace. A covenant says what the goal is, what the terms are, and what the results will be from either fulfilling or dissolving the agreement.

In the Bible, God makes covenants with those He trusts, hoping to bring them closer to Himself. He makes them with Adam, Noah, Abraham, Moses, Joshua, David, and then Jesus. Each time God initiates a covenant, and His followers accept it, He closes the gap a little more between Himself and His people.

Some theologians have suggested picturing a ladder going from Genesis 3 at the bottom (the Fall), up to Revelation 22 (new heavens & earth) at the top. Something like this:

Covenant Ladder of Redemption

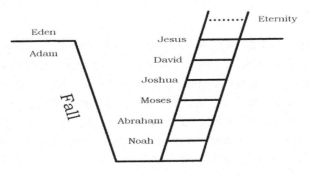

The Bible is the story of God regaining what He lost, one step at a time. He lost His most important thing (relationship) through man, but then uses man to get it back. Each covenant helps humanity take one more step up the ladder until paradise is regained.

Interestingly, the word "testament" actually means "covenant." The "Old Testament" is a chronicle of the "old covenants" that God made with individuals who sought Him. They offered particular blessings like land, sons, or peace.

The "New Testament" is the "new covenant" God made with the world through Jesus. It was His last and best offer through one Man who sought Him completely. It offered free and complete redemption for everyone through the Cross.

But why did redemption have to be progressive? Couldn't God have just jumped man right up to the top of the ladder after the Fall? God could not do that because sin had a deep effect. The whole nature of man and what he wanted was altered—he didn't want God anymore, or holiness. He was stained all the way through and loving what leads to death. (In the fallen state, he still does!)

So God wooed man. He took gradual steps with some people who loved Him and showed faith from their hearts. He invited them and their descendants to come up to a higher place. In other words, sin changed *man* when he fell—not God. God's covenants were a sign of His goodness because on our own, we wouldn't have sought God or known we needed rescuing. God reached out anyway, to rescue us just because we are His children and He wants us to be with Him forever.

Each time that He made a new covenant, God took as big a step as man had the faith for, plus a little more. If He'd tried to rescue us all at once or send Jesus earlier, He would have either had to settle for a very small family in heaven, or He would have had to drag many people there against their will. God didn't want either of these. He dealt with sin in stages so more and more people would come, and come willingly, from the heart.

God restores mankind to Himself through covenants, but He redeems mankind through the Blood. The grand theme of God winning His people back through the blood of Christ has sometimes been called the "scarlet thread." The scarlet thread is a story of *atonement* which weaves its way through the entire Bible.

Every covenant, every step forward in the redemption process, was ratified in sacrificial blood – hence, the "scarlet." Starting with Adam and Eve in the Garden, where God commits the first sacrifice and clothes them with animal skins, the story of sacrificial blood continues through the Old Testament. You see it in the ram which was provided to Abraham so Isaac would live; you see it in the Passover, where sacrificial blood keeps the Hebrews from destruction. The concept of atonement begins in Genesis and develops, as does God's intervening in history to usher people closer.

Eventually, this culminates in the greatest covenant of all, the New Covenant, where God sacrifices Himself and sheds His *own* blood to ratify the covenant and save mankind. The Cross therefore isn't just the central event of being a Christian, it is the central event of the whole Bible. It is the main thing God was revealing the entire time. As Revelation 13:8 reveals, the Lamb was slain *before* the foundations of the world. The Bible is revealing that to us, as it goes along.

Continuity in Two Testaments. This is an important point because, at first glance, the Old and New Testaments appear very different from one another. The mood of God seems different. But God didn't insert Jesus into the story from out of nowhere. Nor did He scatter elements of Jesus' final atonement around in the Old Testament just for us to say, "Oh, that's neat... Jesus is in the Passover."

God was *amplifying* His intervention the entire time. He preached the gospel in Genesis, and it is fulfilled in Revelation. The Bible's redemption story should be seen as one continual revelation, not as two different books pasted into one.

But how, if they are so different? The Old Testament chronicles the redemption story in God's first chosen people, the nation of Israel. God tries to lead them out of the world and into becoming holy followers of Him—through *faith* in the *sacrificial blood* which they offer regularly. This phase of history ends with so many forsaking this faith (or adulterating it) that God cannot help Israel survive past a certain point. The nation implodes, scattering Jewish believers across the Mediterranean.

The New Testament continues the redemption story with a remnant of believing Israel whom God tells that their faith is enough. He is doing away with the other Hebrew requirements to re-open relationship with anyone who can accept His sacrifice by faith. The New Testament makes clear that the Old Testament saints were saved by this *same* faith—by faith in the Messiah and coming sacrifice that would resurrect them at a time they could not see (1 Peter 1:10-12, Hebrews 11:8-17).

In other words, whether you are in the Old or New Testament doesn't matter—both are about God's proactive and loving rescue. Both are about redemption through faith in Jesus' blood (the predetermined sacrifice of God Himself). On the surface, the Old Testament appears different from the New Testament because the Jews were a real nation with a Temple, priesthood, and law code, while Christians don't have any of those.

But both Testaments chronicle the redemptive mission of God inviting a family to leave the lost and dying world with its lusts and pleasures, and to come live with Him. They both invite us to take part in building a heavenly kingdom which will never pass away. As Augustine described it, "What is in the Old Testament concealed, is in the New Testament revealed." Redemption through the blood is one thing that links them.

REDEMPTION IN CREATION

God's love for His lost family is profound and starts from the very beginning. It doesn't take long from the initial creation of mankind for things to go wrong and for God to interrupt with the solution. All the elements of the gospel and God's redemption plan happen right in the first chapters of Genesis.

The Garden. We imagine the Garden of Eden was a place of lush vegetation and perfect weather, but what made it paradise was that Adam and Eve dwelt there in perfect fellowship with their Father. God's presence was tangible, and He walked with them in the cool of the day.

But when Adam and Eve sin, they reject God's voice in favor of Satan's voice. Voice goes with authority; they reject God's authority in favor of Satan's authority, and God's nature in favor of Satan's nature. As a result, they get the "knowledge of good and evil" they ate the fruit of, but this knowledge shows them that they themselves are now evil. So they run, hide, and cover themselves.

God in His love does not allow them to stay in their sin. He comes looking for them and confronts them. This is the God we meet over and over again in the Bible – the one who comes looking, the one who always purses with love in response to evil. Adam and Eve lie to Him, but He exposes their lie and gives them a choice: will they take off their own covering, and put on His instead?

Their covering had been plants and leaves, but in order to make His covering, God has to kill an animal and take its skin. Before their very eyes, Adam and Eve see how truly horrible their sin is. It cannot be neatly covered by human effort but is deserving of death and can only be covered with a sacrifice—done by God. God Himself is able to deal with sin, but they are not.

The gospel is therefore preached in a nutshell—God sacrifices and atones for sin through innocent blood even while man barely knows what he has done wrong.

What Adam and Eve lost through sin was not only their place of authority, but they lost the place of perfect fellowship. God expels them from the Garden, guarding the way back by fire, because man cannot reenter the Garden on his own; the only hope is for God to provide a new way and for them to choose to accept it.

God curses the ground because of them, and possibly because of the serpent that crawled upon it. But they are not without hope. God promises that the seed of the woman will overcome the serpent and bruise his head—in the end, there will be victory.

Cain and Abel. Adam and Eve, now out in the world, have two sons and the two sons bring two kinds of offerings. The first son, Cain, brings the exact same kind of offering that God had already rejected—plants. The second son, Abel, brings the kind of offering that God Himself provided—an animal sacrifice.

God tries to get Cain to repent, but rather than do the right thing by killing an animal, Cain kills his own brother. He does not want God's covering, He wants His own covering. Cain kills an innocent man—a foreshadowing of Christ's execution to come. Then he is, ironically, banned from farming and expelled as a restless wanderer on the earth.

The dynamics in the Garden are therefore the same ones that will play out for the rest of history: man rejects God through choosing sin, but God responds with love and redemption to try to save him from sin and its curse.

REDEMPTION IN THE FLOOD

The sin that begins with Adam and Eve and progresses through Cain begins to deepen and spread as his descendants become the first enemies of the Lord. Yet, God does not allow Cain's evil to triumph over righteous Abel completely. He mercifully provides a third son, Seth, to carry on the seed of righteousness. Jesus' ancestry will trace back to Seth.

After more than 1000 years, the line of Cain manages to corrupt the whole earth. Each generation, supported by lifespans of hundreds of years, simply multiples evil upon itself. Everyone moves farther from God to the point where society's thoughts are wicked all the time. For the sake of a righteous kingdom which has yet to be born, God has to remove all evil from the earth.

Noah. There is only one righteous man with the heart of Abel on the whole earth—Noah. They are not perfect, but God shows Noah, his family, and the animals mercy and gives Noah incredible instructions on how to build an ark of salvation exactly right.

Just as in the Garden, God initiates and intervenes in response to man's sin. God has to create the vessel which can make it through the punishment for sin. Noah can't save his family from destruction by building just any boat he imagines; the world cannot be saved by people trying to avoid it any way they want. Also, no other boat will survive the flood of judgment, only those on God's ark will. This foreshadows how God will provide the narrow way to salvation that many will reject.

Accordingly, Noah obeys and the plan works. The ark is loaded, including with clean animals for proper sacrifices, and the Lord shuts the door. Outside, the world is torn apart. But Noah passes safely through the destruction. Having made it through judgment, Noah gets out and starts over. He and the earth have been born again.

Noah becomes a second kind of Adam, the father of all living. God recommissions him just as He had commissioned Adam: He tells him to be fruitful and multiply, and to take dominion over the earth. Noah also inherits the covenant with Adam, but now God makes a second covenant and promises never to flood the world again.

God tells Noah to build an altar to sacrifice and begin again, making him a priest for the whole world to come. Everyone ever born would be under the blood of this covenant of peace. God sends a rainbow as a sign of His promise and the second creation begins with all succeeding generations coming from the priestly line of Noah. This shows God's desire to have a universal priesthood of believers, and the chance for all to have royal blood.

The New Testament calls the Flood a "baptism" of the world in water (1 Pet. 3:20-21), in hopes that the person who will rise out of the judgment will be one committed to following God's way, cleansed of wickedness. The world which was marred by sin was baptized and established on a new foundation—a supernatural foundation where everything evil perished but God preserved the righteous.

Interestingly, God institutes the death penalty on the renewed earth to protect the world from those who will rise up with a heart of Cain. While it is a stiff punishment, it shows God's firm determination that the world not be entirely corrupted again. Through the ark and the new laws given to Noah, the ladder of redemption grows. God moves forward His plan to save the whole earth through His coming Son.

DISPELLING BABYLON

Although God moves His plans forward, many of the same dynamics are still in place, and history repeats itself.

Only one day after the covenant is established, Noah gets drunk and his son Ham removes his covering. Adam had been a righteous man whose his son rejected God's method of covering sin; now Noah is the second Adam whose sin needs covering yet his son rejects it. The power of choice is evident as the two Adams and the two sons choose unwisely, reflecting their inner hearts towards God.

And just as God responded to Cain's sin with a curse, He responds to Ham's sin with a curse. Ham's son, Canaan, and his descendants become the new enemies of the Lord where Cain's descendants left off. But this time, there are two good sons who survive to offset the curse—the Abel casualty does not repeat.

The Tower of Babel. The descendants of Ham bring the people of the world together at Babel to build a tower so high it aims for heaven. It is a tower that will be the center of man-made religion. Instead of filling and subduing the earth as God had commanded them—showing their obedience to God—it will unify people all in one place and make them so famous they believe the Lord Himself will come down to pay homage to them—making the Lord obey them.

They begin to build the city, a City of Man rather than a City of God. It is a giant act of rebellion, very similar to the process which filled the earth with wickedness the first time. In the same way, the imaginations of the people were wicked in combination with each other (Gen. 6:5, 11:6). This time, God confuses their language to prevent them from further unifying in evil, and to force them to go out and fill the whole earth.

The sad side effect of this is that instead of being united in hate against God, they begin to be divided against one another. Starting in Genesis 10, different nationalities, ethnicities, and tensions begin. Man is at war with one another continually. God stops them from building the City of Man, but who will establish the City of God?

ESTABLISHING ANOTHER CITY

Hundreds of years later, after people had been dispersed from Babel, we learn about a man who lived in the same area where the tower was built. He is a citizen of Babylon who, inside the City of Man, is not satisfied.

Abraham. In his heart, Abraham is "looking for a city whose architect and builder was God" (Heb. 11:10). So Abraham sets out to escape Babylon and find a new land—a place that God Himself will show him and give him.

Something significantly different starts with this man. For the first time, we see a person who really walks with God. By faith, Abraham leaves Babylon and sets out across the Middle East. By faith he accepts God's promise to give him the land of Canaan. By faith he believes that he will have a son in his very old age. And by faith he believes his offspring will become a nation of blessing after him. The Lord makes a covenant with Abraham, showing him how redemption and restoration will advance on the earth through him.

Twenty-five years later, God appears again to Abraham, telling him to walk blameless and be circumcised. For a 99-year old man, circumcision is no small thing, but God wants a physical reminder in blood to show the covenant has been made, as well as sign that his offspring will be set apart. Circumcision is a physical act which sets the Jews apart from other people and signifies how the Messiah will come from their line—specifically, through Isaac and his descendants. So, Abraham circumcises himself and his household.

Interestingly, it is not only Abraham's family who is circumcised, but his Gentile servants are too. This is an amazing picture of God's long-range plan. Although the rest of the Old Testament will be about God fulfilling the promise to Abraham through the nation of Israel, what God actually promises Abraham is that He will make him the father of many nations. The rest of the world, like the Gentile servants, will be grafted in under the same covenant.

This story is put on pause shortly after Genesis 12, but the New Testament will pick it back up and revisit how these other nations will be brought in. Peter initially thinks the Gentiles will be brought in by becoming Jews as well, by being physically circumcised, but Paul makes it clear that what counts is a "circumcised heart" (Rom. 2:29). Spiritually, as "sons of Abraham" (Gal. 3:7), the Church is commissioned to bless all nations of the world through Jesus and therefore fulfill the terms of the "everlasting" covenant God made with Abraham (Gen. 17:7, 8, 13, 19).

The climax of Abraham's walk with God is sacrificing his promised son Isaac, whom he waited his entire life for. God tells Abraham to put Isaac on the altar and sacrifice him. This was not a mean trick. Abraham obeyed because he reasoned in his heart that God would raise Isaac from the dead (Heb. 11:19). It is even possible that, in a prophetic sense of Jesus to come, Abraham believed that a resurrected Isaac would be how God would fulfill his promise and bless all the nations of the earth through him. God was establishing a line of people who would not live by the natural, but were dead to the natural and would live unto God.

In Abraham's mind, Isaac was dead for three days as they made the fateful climb to Mount Moriah (Gen. 22.4). Then God provided a ram to sacrifice in Isaac's place. All this happened in the same region where 2000 years later, God would offer up His own beloved Son!

After Isaac is saved, Isaac becomes the father of the physical nation of Israel, just as Jesus becomes the father of a new spiritual nation of Israel.

OUR LEGACY

God's covenant was made with Abraham, but the establishment or rejection of the covenant is up to Isaac. This is the same pattern we saw with Adam and Seth, and Noah and Shem—the covenants were made with the fathers but fulfilled by the sons. This means that the promises to Abraham will be given only to the son who follows his way.

When Isaac does, but Ishmael does not, Isaac receives the blessing. God renews the Abrahamic covenant with Isaac, but only one of Isaac's sons, Jacob, chooses to walk with God—Esau does not. Sons represent two choices which can be made. Later we see this pattern with Moses and Joshua, David and Solomon, and the Father and His Son. The father gets the challenge from God and the promise of universal blessing, but the son must choose to walk in the ways of his father or the blessings do not come.

Notably, Moses' biological sons and David's sons (other than Solomon) are not the inheritors of their promises. Throughout the Bible, spiritual sons are often grafted in when the firstborn, to whom the birthright belongs, does not respond correctly. This foreshadows that the nation of Israel will reject the gospel (their inheritance), and the Lord will turn to the Gentiles. This pattern forms the heart behind Malachi 4:16, that God wants the hearts of the children to turn to their fathers. Eventually Jesus will serve His Father as the perfect Son, and then all the promises will be obtained.

We walk in this choice today as well, as God's "children" and the "spiritual sons of Abraham" (Galatians 3:6-9). The children of Abraham—the nation of Israel—were supposed to be a beachhead in establishing God's presence on the earth. People all over the world were supposed participate in and extend it.

Since that did not happen, the Old Testament, New Testament, and even today's history is still therefore essentially the fulfillment of God's original promise to Abraham. We are called to walk blamelessly, teaching our children to follow God by faith. We still serve with circumcised hearts to be a blessing to the world. We are still gaining converts and multiplying as the sand on the seashore.

Therefore, Abraham's promises have multiple and increasing fulfillments. First to him as a single individual, then to his biological descendants as Israel, and finally to the whole world through the Church. God fulfilled the promises to Abraham personally by giving him land in Canaan and a son miraculously. God then gave Abraham's biological descendants the entire land of Canaan at the crossroads of the world. Finally, through Christ, God gives Abraham's spiritual descendants victory in all the nations of the world.

The covenant with Abraham becomes the way God fulfills His original purposes in the Garden, to take dominion over the whole earth and let His glory shine through us.

Chapter 8:
Themes in the History of Israel

Abraham was given a promise and a son, but in order to fulfill the promise of a nation coming from him, something more had to happen.

Joseph. Abraham's great-grandson, Joseph, rises to be second-in-command of all of Egypt. This is the world's greatest power at that time, and a wicked nation established by the children of Ham.

For God to fulfill His purposes, simply ruling *over* the world would not suffice. God needed to bring His people *out of the world*. But the Hebrews become enslaved to it. For 400 years, they groan under Egyptian pharaohs who oppress them, just as the followers of Christ groan today when they are under ungodly rulers. God had forewarned Abraham that this would happen. He also had promised they would emerge triumphant, plundering the riches of Egypt.

MOSES AND THE CREATION OF A NATION

Moses. God raises up a deliverer to lead Isaac's descendants out of Egypt. 1500 years later, God would raise up a Deliverer to lead all people out of the world system. Moses is a type of Christ, becoming deliverer and lawgiver for Israel just like Jesus would become Deliverer and Lawgiver for the whole world.

Moses is almost killed when he is born because Pharaoh ordered all Hebrew boys to be killed at birth. Jesus would almost be killed when He was born because King Herod would order the killing of Hebrew baby boys too. Just as Moses is saved as a baby by passing through the wilderness into the house of Pharaoh, Jesus was saved as a baby, by passing into Egypt. Parallels continue throughout Moses' life.

Moses grows up strong and well-educated, but he commits the same mistake Cain before him committed—he tries to please God his own way and ends up a murderer needing to flee his homeland. Like Cain, this leads Moses into the wilderness.

But unlike Cain, Moses repents and is brought back to the place of God's presence. For the first time since the Garden, a man encounters not an angel, but the direct and supernatural presence of God. And just as the pathway to the Garden was guarded by an angel with the flaming sword, God reveals Himself to Moses as a burning bush. God wants to return His consuming presence to earth.

Empowered by God, Moses goes back to confront Pharaoh, the ruler of darkness, to lead the people of God out from under his authority. Pharaoh throws everything he has at Moses but is not able to defeat him.

Pharaoh stubbornly refuses to let God's people go, so God sends a plague against Egypt's firstborn sons. All throughout Genesis, the firstborn symbolizes the image and glory of man who often rejects the image and glory of God. Adam's first son Cain rebelled against God. Abraham's first son Ishmael was rejected. Isaac's firstborn Esau sold his birthright. Now in their rebellion, a whole nation of Egypt is hardened so God destroys all of the firstborns.

And just as Isaac was saved by the blood of a sacrificial lamb, Abraham's descendants are saved by painting lamb's blood on their doors—the Passover. With this plague Pharaoh is defeated, so he releases the people of God. With one last apocalyptic rallying, Pharaoh attempts to reclaim them as they run, but Moses parts the waters for them and they cross over to safety on dry ground. For the first time in the Bible, the people of God have defeated the world—but not with swords, with God's supernatural power. It is a pattern for the future.

The Israelites are now free from bondage! Their enemy's society, religion, and army are utterly destroyed. But like so many who get freed, the Israelites will soon give in to temptation, which comes to lure them back into slavery.

The Wilderness. As the Israelites wander in the desert, they complain about everything. They grumble against Moses, openly rebel under Korah, worship the golden calf, and complain about the bread from heaven because it isn't exciting. It is too hard to follow God, they think. They announce that despite the miracles God has done, they would rather go back and be slaves in Egypt.

Their complaining keeps them wandering in circles in the wilderness for forty years on what should have been an eleven-day journey. Miracles happen all around them and God takes care of their every need, but they can't see the prize before them. The Promised Land is not real to them yet. God leads them with fire by night and a cloud of glory by day, but they have no real hope for where they're going. Even Moses falters and fails to enter the Promised Land.

This greatly grieves the Lord, but He still demonstrates mercy. He gives them water from a rock, quail from a wind, and keeps their clothes and sandals intact. He even gives them the symbol of sin's defeat on the Cross—the serpent on the staff—to save them from death. He pushes them closer to the gospel even in the midst of their resistance.

So many of the events in this period are relevant to us today and illustrate the redemption God is giving us! Let it inspire us to make good choices for Him, and love where we're going even while we don't yet see it.

THE LAW

The Law is another way God pushes Israel closer to the gospel. It is fashionable to see the Law as outdated, oppressive, prior to the gospel, and perhaps even in opposition to it. But Jesus says the Law was a "tutor" to lead us to Him (Gal. 3:24-25). He says that He fulfilled the Law, not abolished it. The Law was not bad; it was just not good enough.

God makes a covenant with Israel on Mt. Sinai and, as the sign of this agreement, gives them the Law. Moses descends with the Ten Commandments and tells them that these moral principles will bring them into right standing with God.

The people, however, seeing the awesomeness of God from the mountain, do not want a relationship with this Lord. As the lightning and thunder crash around, they tell Moses they don't want God to speak to them. Instead they want a mediator (Ex. 20). They tell him they would rather have rules and laws than direct access. It seems hard to believe, but arguably this choice has plagued the people of God all the way through history, up to the present!

Moses begs the Israelites to choose relationship with the living God, but they stay away from the mountaintop. They get what they asked for—a formal priesthood and a system of mediation where they don't have to be responsible for their own walk with God. They can have others make atonement for them, abstain from some things, celebrate some holidays, and be good to go.

The first part of what God gives them is the civil law. The civil law contains all the instructions for building a successful society. It includes the Ten Commandments, an ethical code upon which societies flourish for years. It also includes rules about washing, farming, trading, relationships, children, strangers, even taking care of the poor. All kinds of mundane matters a society would need to know, God includes in the civil law to bless them.

God also establishes the ceremonial and religious laws, which govern how they will worship. Starting with Moses' brother, Aaron, there were to be priests between God and man who would be set apart by obeying special standards. The priests would then make sure sacrifices were performed correctly, with the blood of unblemished, firstborn male animals as the closest substitute to Christ. God explains how to deal with the sacrificial flesh and the blood correctly because each is a significant part of the atonement that foreshadows Jesus.

Additionally, God institutes the Sabbath, the feasts and festivals, and the year of Jubilee so that His people's consciences would be trained to think about Him consistently and correctly—i.e. as a God of forgiveness, thanksgiving, and restoration. The laws reflect God's nature, so knowing them is a little like knowing Him. It isn't a substitute for encountering Him personally, but the people receive a system where they can relate to God through obedience, liturgy, and regularity.

Lastly, God gives Moses the exact instructions for building a tent called the Tabernacle, which was a place God Himself could dwell. God wanted to move in! Constructing a new ark of salvation, the Ark of the Covenant, the priests place this in a sacred place, the Holy of Holies. Here, the high priest entering annually could find forgiveness for all people at the Mercy Seat, a shadow of Christ's throne.

The Law ends up rather long. It is a peace treaty where if the Israelites do the things God commands—build the Tabernacle, complete the sacrifices, and follow the law code—He can bless them. But it is a way to secure God's blessing upon their nation without them questioning their own hearts. It is a covenant of works because that's what they want. God lays out exactly the things they need to do to be approved, but it hard to get further than that.

On the other hand, these concepts were all new to the people of God and did give them important truths that would bless them. They were especially different from the Egyptian religion the Jews had been immersed in for hundreds of years prior. Through the Law, the Lord begins to advance His redemptive plan. He separates His people from the world, and so is able to bring them slightly closer to Himself.

For some time now, both Jews and Christians have stumbled over how the Law fits into God's plan of redemption. How and why could God create something which was meant to pass away? The answer is that the Law was not the long-term redemptive plan of God, but was the method He used to prepare a people to receive His long-term plan, Jesus' atonement.

After exiting Egypt, the Israelites weren't ready to walk holy before the Lord yet. They were still yearning for their old worldly system. So God gave them a better one—He took away their old fig leaf covering and gave them a new one that was salvation through atonement. In this way, the Lord was able to take slaves who still longed for Egypt and turn them into a rich, powerful, internally strong nation, using the Law.

Today we are conditioned to see the Law as oppressive so that its blessing is not immediately apparent. But we have two thousand years of Christian civilization behind us, so it's easy to take a good society for granted. The Israelites had nothing. God needed a tool, and His tool was the civil, ceremonial, and sacrificial laws. They formed a kind of divine User's Manual which, if they followed, would lead to a nation that would bless and be blessed, just as God had promised Abraham.

The Law accomplished several things. First, it kept the Israelites in communion with God. It provided a structure to keep the entire nation free from sin, which meant God could stay near them to guide them, advise them, and bless them. The general population had never had that before. They had never had forgiveness, or a way to close the gap between themselves and God. They probably didn't even know they needed it. They had had only idolatry and spiritual bondage before.

The Law also provided a "guardrail" to keep God's people set apart from the rest of the world. In order for Jesus to come into the world, He was prophesied to come from the loins of Abraham, but that was going to be tricky. Remember how quickly after Seth all of mankind became corrupt except for one man, Noah? After Noah, society quickly disintegrated again until God called another man, Abraham.

The Law made sure this wouldn't happen again. It set Israel apart and formed a group of people with a conscience submitted to God. It created a protective pool of people where the Messiah could emerge from, and it primed those people to recognize the Messiah when He came. In a sense, it was to prepare out of a wilderness a Garden for God to come live on earth and take dominion. This is why Paul said it was a blessing for the Jews to have been given the patriarchs, covenants, Law, and temples (Romans 9:4-5). These were all pointers to salvation.

But Paul also said the Law was a curse, added because of transgression (Gal. 3:18). How could it be both? Because the Law was meant to convict. It was created to bring the world under judgment and condemn it for falling short (Romans 3:19-25). Without it, no-one would know they were guilty and needing salvation. They would think that they were good, and God was evil, if He didn't accept them—just as many believe today. The Law showed that the truth is the other way around. It held up a mirror to show people that they were not good. They needed a good, saving God.

To those who did not let the Law convict them, it became a stumbling stone. The scribes and Pharisees idolized the Law rather than the One who wrote it, so to them, the blessing became a curse.

It wasn't a curse because the content of the Law was bad—building a society on God's moral code was a blessing. It was a curse because relating to Him through rules and regulations was not a blessing. God really wanted to bring mankind into His presence without a covenant of works. Paul said the Law was a "tutor to Christ" because it was a stepping stone that God meant to replace with something better (Gal. 3:24). It laid the foundation for knowledge of sin, the need for salvation, and all the higher ethics Jesus would teach.

To understand how this works in real life, think of how it plays out in child-raising. When your children are young, you give them rules they need to obey. They are not capable of receiving heart-level principles to change and become someone different. The process of raising children under rules, however, convicts them of sin in important places and shapes them into healthy people. Then they can learn harder, heart-level truths because they can receive them, value them, want them. The real purpose of your rules was not outward obedience. It was heart-level obedience which can only happen when they get older.

In the same way, the Law helped Israel be convicted of sin so that they would eventually be able to hear the real gospel, which is based on the forgiveness of sin but also the foundation of what that is and why it is bad. Learning to "be good" helped them get to the place where they could grow and get in real relationship with God and others—the essence of the Cross.

This is what Paul meant when he said the Law was a tutor to Christ. He meant the Jews weren't in the dark like the pagans were, and had the proper foundation to build a relationship with God.

The Law was therefore the next step in God's rescue plan for the earth. It was designed to show the way, but not be the way. It was designed to expose the futility of human salvation and prepare the way for the better covenant Jesus would bring (Hebrews 8).

When Jesus came, His new covenant made the Law obsolete because in His flesh He abolished its ministry of death (Ephesians 2:11-18). All the things prior to the Law—Abraham's walk by faith, his circumcision, his communion, the tithe—all get incorporated into the Church as they are reinterpreted by the Cross (Romans 4). But no-one today, not even the Jews, practice the Law as in the days of Moses. The Law was meant to be a parenthesis in God's plan of redemption. It was meant to be a tutor to salvation by faith—which, just like a tutor, we give up when we mature.

ESTABLISHING ISRAEL

Israel's relationship to the Lord in the next phase of history is rocky, but God still chooses to draw them closer. This shows His unconditional love.

In the last era, the nation of Israel did not have the heart to obey and trust God as Abraham, Isaac, and Jacob had. They were tested in the wilderness and they failed, so God did not allow them to reap the benefit of the covenant—the Promised Land. He had promised this to Abraham over 500 years earlier. An entire generation died in the wilderness until a new generation led by Joshua and Caleb had faith to take possession of the Land.

Joshua and Caleb. Joshua and Caleb believe God for the awesome promise of a home. Joshua had been Moses' aide since he was young and camped near the tent where Moses met with God. When the new generation of Israelites stand at the brink of Canaan, God renews the Mosaic covenant with Joshua. He promises that they will win the whole territory and be blessed if they obey, just as He promised Abraham and Moses.

God also repeats the incredible miracle of parting the sea at the Jordan River to show that Joshua and this next generation are going to start right where Moses left off. He orders Joshua to circumcise all the men after crossing the river, and appears to him as an angel, asking him to take his shoes off on holy ground.

But God adds something to this new covenant just to reward Joshua's own faith and courage. God prophesies particular blessings over each tribe of Israel. He tells them that they will have victory over their enemies and be placed high above all other nations.

After that, Joshua has amazing success in war, conquering the Canaanites who lived in the Promised Land. But like all covenants with God, the obedience factor is still the catch. God really wants to give the Israelites a place of their own, but not just any place—a place for the Kingdom of God. It is meant to be a light to the nations, so only a people of faith and obedience will be able to obtain this precious possession and keep it.

Accordingly, this new covenant stipulates that if the people become disobedient and seek other gods, curses will fall upon them: famine, disease, defeat, etc. God warns them that walking outside His covenant will leave them vulnerable and cause them to experience all the consequences of sin. Most importantly, they will lose the Promised Land if disobedience continues. This is exactly what will happen to Israel in the future, by the time King Solomon's reign is over.

Right away, the nation of Israel experiences ups and down in their walk. For a little over a decade, Joshua leads the campaign to conquer the Promised Land and repossess it from the Canaanites. He is successful and the Levites are given 48 cities scattered throughout the territory so that their godly behavior can influence all the people. What a beautiful picture of the priests of God, in each of their locales, permeating a culture!

But battles continue as Israel's tribes settle in their regions and slowly displace the native peoples. In some places, Israel begins to adopt pagan practices, and the cycles of obedience and disobedience begin.

The nation falls into sin, worshipping idols like Baal and Asherah. They start to experience the curses of disobeying the covenant. They then cry out for a deliverer. God sends them one, a Judge, who conquers enemy people groups and initiates a period of freedom. Then Israel relapses and starts the cycle again.

Ups and Downs with the Judges. During the period of the Judges, approximately 400 years, this sequence happens at least twelve times. God in His mercy keeps letting them try again. Also during this time, Israel had no official king because it was supposed to be a nation whose ruler was the Lord (Joshua 8:23). But the relapses cause so much trouble that they are pushed towards needing a king, at least from their viewpoint. God makes it clear that this pathway is not His first choice for them.

Had the Israelites not cycled through obedience and disobedience so many times, it is likely the Lord's promise to have victory over their neighbors would have been fulfilled quickly and easily. But by 1000BC, the conquest of Canaan which had begun 400 years earlier under Joshua was still not complete. Israel was still flirting with their enemies' gods.

By the end of the period of the Judges, all of Israel was doing whatever they thought was right in their own eyes (Judges 21:25). Consecration to the Lord had fizzled.

Still, the acquisition of a homeland was God's redemptive plan moving forward. The Israelites are at least settled in the territory and the Tabernacle is built in Shiloh. There is at least a small beachhead established for God's will to come forth on the earth.

A Kingdom under Saul. The Israelites cry out for a king to help them finish up the job of conquering Canaan, but King Saul is not a good representative of God. The forty years under him is a kind of spiritual wandering as he unites all tribes under one kingdom but does not follow the Lord's will closely. He is impetuous, competitive, and jealous, and falls into the same trap as Cain—trying to conduct the sacrificial offering the way he wants without proper procedure. This leads to a curse on his reign. The prophet and last Judge, Samuel, declares that his rule will be torn from him and given to another.

REDEMPTION UNDER KING DAVID

God chooses David, a man after His own heart, under whom His will can pour forth. Samuel anoints David as just a young man, a shepherd who immediately makes his faith in God known when he defeats the giant Goliath with a single stone. This is a symbol of Jesus' meek yet effective conquest of the Antichrist and enemies of the Lord.

Later David's heartfelt devotion to God is seen through all the prayers and psalms he writes. More than anyone, David is the forerunner who models how to praise and worship Him. The inner workings of His mind also prophetically reflect the thoughts of Christ; Jesus quotes the Psalms more than any other Old Testament book.

It is the first time in the Old Testament that the concept of God as intimately personal and loving comes forth. David reveals it in faith; he knows who he walks with. With Abraham you saw God's generosity, and with Moses you saw God's power. But with David, God's desire to be communing with you in the early morning hours, in every waking thought, is finally known. God wants to be close enough to His people for them to really see His heart, and for them to know God really accepts theirs.

Correspondingly, David's rule brings God's people closer to Him. David returns His presence to them in the form of the Ark of the Covenant, which had been carried off by the Philistines. Once it is back in the Tabernacle, God makes a new covenant with David—the next rung on the ladder of redemption. He promises Israel victory in all their military campaigns, as well as peaceful settlement. He swears by the sun, moon, and stars that David will have a king on the throne forever.

This is a big deal because up until that point, the nation of Israel had been very unsteady. There was still doubt over whether the kingdom was going to work out at all. But when God promises this to David, the Jews hear their nation and kingdom will last forever. They have renewed confidence that God is with them.

On the other side of the Cross, we know their physical kingdom will not last forever—it will be conquered in the next 500 years—but the spiritual kingdom does last, and God brings the Messiah out of David's line to rule the world forever.

In the meantime, God blesses the reign of David and solidifies the conquest of the Promised Land under him. David is the beloved king of a united Israel for 40 years, ushering in a Golden Age of peace and prosperity. God even shows mercy and patience with future kings who stray from Him, just because of their father David. You see David's flaws but you also see there is nothing God won't forgive or do through those who stand like a rock for Him.

God then declares He is ready to move in! Now that Israel is settled, God commands the construction of the Temple which will settle His presence too. From there, He will rule over, protect, and forgive all His people. This has been His heart since the very beginning—it is getting closer to being actualized. God doesn't allow David himself to build His house because David has been a man of war his whole life, but He promises David's son Solomon the job, and gives him the blueprint for building it.

King Solomon. Solomon's reign experiences the most blessings as the result of David's devotion. Israel has years of peace and success through trading. Israel becomes the wealthiest and most powerful nation at that time, the envy of the world, giving glory to God's provision.

Solomon has good moments of devotion, such as when he asks the Lord for wisdom rather than riches. But his heart is eventually led astray by his wealth and wives. He builds heathen altars and ruins the purity of faith that was so zealously guarded by David. After his 40 years, the kingdom divides and is never the same again.

REDEMPTION THROUGH THE PROPHETS

After approximately 1000 years of building up covenants between Abraham and David, there is approximately 1000 years of Israel breaking them down between David and Jesus. There are no more Old Testament covenants made after David, but God's devotion to

His people is still evident in the history following. Mainly, His redemptive heart is seen through His servants, the prophets. They become His mouthpiece and the conscience of the nation.

After Solomon's reign, the plan for God's will to spread on earth is stalled. So is His desire to commune with His people, due to how Israel is led astray by idols and wicked kings. There is no-one pulling the nation back to its roots and the original promises except the prophets.

Throughout the next 500 years, God sends prophets to both northern and southern kingdoms of Israel to call them back to Himself. Their messages are all basically the same: return to your first love, the true and pure worship of God, and you will be restored.

Not many kings listen to this call, but God keeps sending the message. A few times, God even sends it to pagans, the Gentiles of His time! For example, Nineveh, the capital of Assyria and enemy of the Jews, repents under Jonah and experiences a temporary revival. Through this you see how God pronounces judgment on the nations oppressing Israel, but His love for them is still great.

Throughout the age of the prophets, God has harsh words for Israel floundering in deep idolatry but continues to hope for them. One third of the book of Isaiah, for example, is devoted to blessing Israel and the Messianic age to come.

Jeremiah too represents the heart of the Lord as he weeps over Israel's coming destruction under the Babylonians—that is God weeping with them. Up until the very last moment, Jeremiah is with Israel and prophesying to his last breath—that is God holding out hope for them.

Ezekiel actually lives in exile in Babylon, extending faith to the Lord's people—that is the Lord with His people. Daniel acts on the Lord's behalf from within Babylon, and Esther intercedes for God's people to be saved while in Persia. The Lord never abandons His first love even though they continue to abandon Him. He is with them in the midst of their rebellion, calling them back to Himself.

REDEMPTION AFTER THE EXILE

After Israel is released from captivity, the chroniclers of the exile become fixated on why the nation of Israel was captured when they were given all these amazing promises. The answer is simply that they could not obey the terms of the covenants. One by one, they abandoned the conditions, so one by one, the promises failed to be realized. Finally the Promised Land was lost and they were exiled from the land.

Years later, God is faithful to bring a remnant of Israel back to the land. Nehemiah and Ezra are the story of how God sends people in groups to restore what was lost. The Jews build a second Temple. They confront people who are in the land again. They try to recapture the promise made to Abraham more than 1500 years before.

In between Old and New Testaments. Several hundred years later, around 100BC, Judah (Judea) regains its independence and re-establishes national Israel under the Hasmonean dynasty. The Hasmoneans recognize they no longer have the prophets or the Davidic kingship, but they do have the Law and the priesthood. They begin waiting expectantly for God to restore the Kingdom of God to His people again.

Eventually King Herod arises, builds the Jews a new massive temple—the third Temple—and claims to be the rightful King of the Jews. But Herod was biologically a descendant of Esau, the son who rejected the birthright. It is under this pretender, Herod, that God sends them their real King—a son of David—to fulfill all the promises He ever gave to Israel including another deliverer. This time the offer will extend beyond Israel to the world, with the promise that sin, and then pain, will end forever.

Chapter 9:
New Testament Overview

Many excellent books survey each book of the New Testament, so it is not our aim to repeat that here. Nor can we cover the kind of theology and application which deep studying imparts. But the following will give you some basic orientation to understanding the New Testament.

THE GOSPELS

The New Testament covers approximately 90 years of history, from just prior to Jesus' birth, through His death, to the last revelation of his oldest apostle, John. In comparison to the 2000+ years of Old Testament history, the New Testament outlines a very small section of history.

Jesus' life is told in the account of the four gospels. Put together, they cover the time period from right before His birth to just after His death—a period of about 33 years.

Matthew, Mark, and Luke are called the *"synoptic" gospels* which means "look alike." They have similar wording, similar stories, and similar sequences. The Gospel of John is not one of the synoptic gospels because it has important differences. It focuses on the significance of Jesus' teachings, including long discourses in great depth, rather than just His proverbial sayings or quick interpretations.

Additionally, some material from the synoptic gospels is left out of the Gospel of John, such as the parables and Jesus' casting out demons. Other material that the synoptics omit, John includes, such as the resurrection of Lazarus and Jesus' farewell address (John 13-17). John also includes more years of Jesus' ministry.

At this point, one of the questions people often ask is, why are there four gospels? The simplest answer is that the gospels represent four historical accounts of Jesus. They provide four expert testimonies of people who walked with Him and witnessed His ministry. Through each we get a slightly different perspective on the same life.

Some Bible interpreters have studied this in great detail and come up with interesting observations. Matthew's audience was mostly Jewish so he shares many Old Testament Scriptures and interpretations. Luke is a Gentile historian and shares a lot of Jesus' encounters with Gentiles. Mark is commonly held to be the earliest written gospel and goes through Jesus' life very quickly. John writes in his very old age, approximately 60 years after Jesus lived, and has a very reflective and devotional tone, rather than a historical one.

Another popular school of thought says each gospel author emphasized different themes that God thought was important. For example, Matthew emphasized Jesus as King of the Jews, Mark emphasized Jesus as the suffering servant of God, Luke described Jesus as the servant of man, and John described Jesus as the divine Son of God.

Whether or not these brushstrokes are accurate, the Holy Spirit led four different men to capture a unique picture of Christ. His life could not be attested to by just one exhaustive biography, nor could it be validated or appreciated to its fullest from just one angle.

JESUS' LIFE

Prior to Jesus' arrival, the Jews under Roman government had been yearning for a Messiah. Different schools of thought and political movements had shaped the previous centuries of Judaism, but many still wished for the Kingdom of God to come again. They were following their leaders as best they could but were, as Jesus calls them, "sheep without a shepherd." The voice of God had been silent since the days of Malachi.

Then around 0AD, an angel visits an elderly priest named Zacharias and tells him that he and his wife Elizabeth will have a son. They are to name him John, and John (the Baptist) will have the power of Elijah to turn the hearts of the fathers back to the children. In other words, God says that the fulfillment of the very last promise He spoke through the Prophets is now getting ready to occur. God is ready to move and breathe revelation into His people again.

Several months later, an angel visits Elizabeth's cousin, Mary, and tells her that even though she is virgin, she will bear the Son of God and He will save the world from its sins! Her husband-to-be, Joseph, who is a descendant of King David, almost breaks their engagement. But an angel comes to him in a dream to tell him this is the fulfillment of Messianic prophecy. Joseph wakes and immediately marries Mary.

The young couple journeys to Bethlehem and the Christmas story unfolds. Jesus is born in the city of David. He is born in an unknown place, at an unknown time, to a basically unknown family. But He is born as the Light in the darkness, and everyone who sees Him, from the poor shepherds to the three kings of the East, recognize the truth.

The plot against Jesus' life starts from the moment He is born. King Herod tricks the magi and conspires with the chief priests and scribes to kill Him as a baby. Jesus only escapes because another angel warns Joseph in a dream to flee to Egypt. It's a strange place of refuge, but Scripture tells us that this was to fulfill the Old Testament promise that, "Out of Egypt, I called my son." This has typological fulfillment for us, as God also saves us from our Egypt when we are lost and without Him.

After that, Jesus is left alone to grow in the Spirit and work as a carpenter under Joseph, His father. Jesus does this for thirty years until He is led to the Jordan River and baptized by His cousin, John the Baptist. Heaven is opened at that moment, and those with ears to hear, hear the Father calling out that Jesus is His beloved Son. They also see the Holy Spirit coming down onto Jesus in the form of a dove.

The Holy Spirit leads Jesus into the wilderness where Satan tests Jesus and tries to get Him to kill Himself and abort His ministry. Instead, Jesus defeats Satan with the Word of God. In doing so, He fulfills the tests of faith and obedience originally given to the Israelites when they were trying to exit Egypt but grumbled in the Sinai desert. Jesus succeeds where they failed and takes their place (and our place) as the obedient child of God.

In contrast to Israel, Jesus is given access to the Promised Land right away—an entrance point of God's dwelling on earth—in the form of the power to save. He begins His ministry in the town of Galilee. Even though the people in the synagogue try to throw Him off a cliff, Jesus can't be stopped. He starts healing people, casting out demons, and drawing crowds. Heaven is open!

Jesus then calls twelve disciples—fulfilling the original mission of the twelve tribes of Israel—and starts teaching common people the secrets of heaven. Massive crowds are hungry for truth and they follow Jesus everywhere, all the time. They bring their sick, they climb up mountains to hear Him, they sojourn with Him for days.

Jesus gives people literal bread and spiritual bread (the Word, the truth of God). They can see He is the real manna, the real Bread of Life that will never run out. He breaks bread with them and tells them they will have to eat of His body if they want to be His disciple. He demonstrates that His body and the Word are one and the same; they are our provision and sustenance.

Throughout Jesus' ministry, He goes back and forth from His home base in Galilee to Jerusalem. Each time He is in the capital, He escalates the confrontation with Jewish leadership, which arouses more and more hatred towards Him. On one memorable trip, He turns over the tables of the moneychangers to show that the

Temple is God's house, not a house of the world. He condemns and delegitimizes the Pharisees especially, both their authority and their teachings.

Meanwhile the Romans hate the revolution and disorder. John the Baptist has been arrested and set to be beheaded at the order of Herod's wife. Jesus continues stirring up animosity as He circulates Israel, teaching and performing miracles. He makes initial contact with the Gentile world when He ministers to the woman at the well, and to the Syro-Phoenecian woman, and to the Roman centurion. Jesus' power and authority start to become even more widely known.

When the Transfiguration on the mountain occurs, it becomes clear who Jesus really is. Peter recognizes Him as Messiah and so do many whom Jesus heals. He sends His disciples out, first two by two, and then sends the seventy to do mighty deeds in His Name. When Jesus raises Lazarus from the grave after three days, it can hardly be doubted that Jesus is not subject to any authority in this life. He is prophesying to them what He will do, which is disarm the devil and all those in league with Him.

Jerusalem is already stirring when Jesus returns to the Temple again, slowly and publicly, riding on a donkey. People wave palm leaves and shout "Hosanna!" (*Save us, Lord!*) It is a sort of humble coronation ceremony. Seeing the challenge to themselves and the Roman government, the High Priest remarks that it would be better for this one man to die than the whole nation of Israel to suffer for treason. Jesus' fate is sealed at that moment.

Judged guilty by His own leaders, and betrayed with a kiss by one of His own disciples, Jesus is arrested in the Garden of Gethsemane after a night of blood, sweat, and tears. He is given a hearing before Annas, a trial before the Sanhedrin, and taken from the Roman governor Pontius Pilate to King Herod, then back to Pilate again.

Jewish leadership condemns Him but gets the Romans to order the actual execution. Pilate doesn't want to be the one to take responsibility but submits to the chanting and pressure from the Jewish crowd, whom the Romans are already worried about controlling. Thinking this will quell the matter, Pilate sentences Jesus to crucifixion.

Jesus is stripped, beaten, whipped, and given a crown of thorns. His punishers divide up His clothes, nail Him to the Cross, and hang Him between two common thieves on Good Friday. The earth is enveloped in darkness as Jesus suffers. He dies at the end of the day.

Then the veil of the Temple dramatically tears in two. Earthquakes erupt, the dead are raised, and everyone is suddenly aware of the magnitude of what they have done. As one Roman witness remarks, they have surely killed the Son of God.

But the story doesn't end there, as we know! On Sunday morning, some of Jesus' followers find His tomb standing empty. One of the angels tells them that He has risen from the dead. They rush back to report the news to the apostles, who return to the gravesite to find nothing but linen graveclothes lying there.

A short time later, Jesus appears to His disciples in His resurrected body. He explains that He has conquered death and risen again. He stays with them for forty days, teaching them about Himself, the Scriptures, and the things to come. He then commissions them to disciple the world in His name, breathes upon them, and ascends back up into heaven. The baton has been passed to the Church! His mission is now ours!

PAUL'S MINISTRY

Jesus' disciples immediately begin their outreach; one small group begins the Great Commission to save the world. Judas commits suicide and is replaced with another apostle. Then Jesus Himself commissions Paul from heaven, in a divine encounter. He asks him to spread the gospel to the Gentile (Greek-speaking) world, starting within the Roman Empire.

One of the hardest things to understand in the New Testament is the ministry of Paul (ca. 35-67AD) because his life's work is not told in a strict chronology anywhere. The book of Acts tells the majority of his story and how the Early Church spreads west, from Jerusalem, mostly due to his mission trips.

In the big picture, Paul takes three missionary journeys around the Greek world, planting churches. He performs miracles and encounters death multiple times, from Gentiles, Jews, and natural disasters. Finally, his enemies get him deported to Rome which turns out to be a mission trip all of its own. While on house arrest there, Paul gets the gospel to permeate the capital city. From Rome, it will eventually spread to the rest of the world. For being just one man, Paul took a huge step in fulfilling the Great Commission!

The book of Acts chronicles Paul's three mission trips prior to his imprisonment in Rome. During these trips, Paul writes his *epistles*—letters from Paul to pastors and churches he helps plant. This means the history told in Acts and the epistles of Paul overlap.

But remember, the epistles are in your Bible according to their length, not according to the order they were actually written, which is the order they are mentioned in book of Acts. Acts forms the template of New Testament history which Paul's epistles can be plugged into.

Many Bibles contain maps of Paul's missionary journeys, but those can be hard to understand. Basically, Paul's missions get bigger each time he goes on one. He goes to some new places but then cycles back through the churches he planted previously.

This makes it hard to pin down exactly when Paul wrote to each church. The date for the book of Galatians, for example, is debatable because Paul visited Galatia three times. It is also hard to pin down where Paul wrote from, since he usually wrote to one church while on his way to another one. This information has to be pieced together carefully from little clues in different books, but there are still some question marks.

The book of Acts is our best source of information about Early Church. It provides a historical account of how the gospel of salvation through faith in Jesus Christ went from belonging to a tiny region in Israel to the entire Gentile world (Acts 1:1-3). This took approximately 35 years, from about 33-68AD, or the time between Jesus' death and Paul's death.

The gospel writer Luke wrote Acts after he wrote his account of Jesus. Luke was a physician and Gentile historian from Antioch who became a leader in the Philippian church. He joined Paul on his travels in Acts 16. He stayed with him until Paul was imprisoned in Rome in Acts 28, so he was a personal eyewitness to most of Paul's ministry.

Year	Event	Scripture	Book Written
35	Paul approves the stoning of Stephen	Acts 7:47-50	
36	Paul's conversion in Damascus and flight to Arabia	Acts 9:1-25 2 Cor 11:32-33 Gal. 1:17	
39	15 days in Jerusalem With Apostles	Acts 9:26-27 Gal. 1:18	
39	Ministry in Syria & Home of Cilicia	Acts 9:30 Gal. 1:21	
44	Spends a year in Antioch	Acts 11:25-26	
45	Second Visit in Jerusalem	Acts 11:27-30, 12:25	
45	**1st Mission Journey** to Cyprus and Galatia w/Barnabas	Acts 13:2-14:28	
50	Council at Jerusalem	Acts 15:1-29	

51	2nd Mission Journey to Greece w/Silas	Acts 15:40-18:23	*Gal.* (from Corinth) *1 & 2 Thess.* (from Corinth)
54	3rd Mission Journey mostly in Ephesus	Acts 18:23-21:1	*1 Cor* (from Ephesus) *2 Cor* (frm Macedonia) *Rom* (from Corinth)
58	Arrested in Jerusalem and Imprisoned in Caesarea	Acts 21:1-26:32	
60	Journey to Rome	Acts 27:1-28:15	
61	Imprisoned in Rome	Acts 28:16-31 Phil. 4:23	Ephesians Colossians Philemon *Philippians* (from Roman prison)
63	Possible mission trip to Spain while on house arrest	Rom. 15:23-29	1 Timothy *Titus* (from Macedonia)
68	Re-Imprisonment, Trial and Execution		*2 Timothy* (from prison)

The chart above contains one of the most common synopses of Paul's life and missionary journeys. It lists the books he wrote from each location, to the extent that that is known.

Many scholars believe that Luke wrote Acts while he was in Rome with Paul, and could get first-hand information from Paul himself. Here is a summary of Luke's account of Paul's life:

Paul, after the death of Christ. Paul was a reputable Pharisee from Tarsus who studied under the prestigious teacher, Gamaliel. He seems to have been a member of the Sanhedrin which condemned Stephen. He could have even been at the Sanhedrin meetings which condemned Jesus and flogged Peter. Scripture says Paul was at Stephen's stoning, giving approval to all that was done (Acts 22:20).

But the last act of Stephen was to pray for his persecutors, which works on Paul. For a little while longer, Paul leads the persecution against the Church, "breathing out murderous threats" (9.1), beating believers, dragging them to prison, and executing them. But as he sets out for Damascus to destroy the church there, the Lord appears to him in a blinding vision and knocks him to the ground.

Paul repents and is healed three days later. He then finishes his trip to Damascus by preaching the gospel instead. What a turnaround! The Jews there and in Jerusalem pursue Paul as a public enemy for several years before Barnabas gets ahold of him and introduces his public ministry to the wider world.

Paul establishes a base at Antioch. Barnabas, the cousin of the gospel author Mark, is sent by Peter and the church in Jerusalem to approve of the Gentile church in Antioch. At some point, Barnabas travels to Tarsus and picks up Paul there. He then persuades the disciples to accept Paul as a real apostle of Jesus Christ.

Barnabas takes Paul to Antioch where Paul gets to flex his wings at being a leader in the new Gentile church. Fortunately for Paul, Antioch takes off and becomes his home base. He starts three of his missionary journeys from there, and returns there after two of them, to give reports.

Galatia with Barnabas—First Missionary Journey. After more than a decade at Antioch, Paul is ready to branch out into the wider Gentile world. He takes Barnabas on his first missionary trip through Galatia (Asia Minor/Turkey). He evangelizes in Cyprus, Psidian Antioch, Iconium, Lystra, and Derbe. Then he returns to his home base.

Some of the important things which happen to Paul on this trip include his name change (from Saul to Paul), the blinding of a sorcerer, and a stoning which leaves Paul for dead.

Another important thing which happens is John Mark's quitting partway through the journey. This causes a temporary falling out between Paul and John Mark. It is possible that Timothy meets Paul at this time, because he was from Lystra. Paul and Barnabas perform many miracles on this trip, witness many salvations, and are chased out of almost every place they go.

Tour of Greece with Silas—Second Missionary Journey. On the second mission trip, Paul takes Silas with him to Greece. This time he and Barnabas have a disagreement because Barnabas wants John Mark to come with them and Paul does not. Paul and Silas end up going to Greece while Barnabas and John Mark go somewhere else.

At one of Paul's first stops, in Lystra, he picks up Timothy who becomes his constant companion from that point. They go to Troas, Philippi, Thessalonica, Berea, Athens, Corinth, and Ephesus before returning home to Antioch.

Some of the important things which happen on this second missionary journey are: the Lord stopping Paul from going to Ephesus, their picking up Luke and dropping him off at Philippi, Paul and Silas escaping from prison in Philippi when God sends an earthquake, their staying over a year to establish the Corinthian church, and their meeting Priscilla and Aquila who host them in various places. This was also the time of Paul's tent-making, which he did to support himself while at Corinth for so long.

Overall, Paul's success in Greece is impressive. He makes many converts in every place except Athens, the seat of Greek paganism and intellectualism. Greece becomes a haven for successful churches, many of whom will receive Paul's epistles. Paul writes the very first letters to the believers in Galatia and Thessalonica.

Ephesian Focus—Third Missionary Journey. Paul's third mission trip is back to where his heart truly lies: Ephesus. This visit seems to have been the climactic event and most fantastic trip in Paul's career. It also held special significance being on the Imperial

Highway to Rome. It influenced many travelers passing through there.

For three years Paul works in Ephesus, preaching day and night and performing special miracles. He is so successful that magicians there start burning their books publicly, up to fifty thousand pieces of silver's worth! (Acts 19:11-20).

The mission is a long one during which Paul manages to return to most of the cities and churches he planted previously. He writes epistles to the Corinthians to correct several problems which arose since he last saw them. He also writes the book of Romans to the believers in Rome. Paul had not been to Rome at that point but was praying that God would make it possible for him to go.

Paul in Jerusalem. Paul had been in and out of Jerusalem before, but never with good results. The Jews there were determined to kill him for his defect to Christianity. Still, Paul is determined to give the church in Jerusalem the offering money he had picked up from the Gentile churches. Those who love Paul plead with him not to go because they think the Jews will kill him this time for sure.

They almost do. Acts 21-23 records how a Jewish mob which recognizes Paul at the Temple rush at him and start beating him to death. The Roman soldiers save him just in time. Paul manages to yell out his testimony from the exact same stairway where Pilate had condemned Jesus to death 28 years before. The mob rushes him again, when he is halfway through. The Roman commander rescues Paul and puts him in a fortress for safekeeping.

The next day, the commander brings Paul back to the Sanhedrin, but chaos breaks out again. They vow to kill him. Paul is brought a second time to the Roman fortress, where the Lord intervenes. Paul's nephew manages to smuggle him out in the middle of the night with a huge entourage.

Paul held in Caesarea. Paul spends two years on house arrest in Caesarea, the Roman capital city of Judah. A basically Romanized city in Israel, Caesarea is the place of Paul's first evangelism to Romans—a preparation phase for the real deal.

For two years, Paul is a prisoner in the Roman governor's palace and ends up witnessing regularly to Felix (the first governor), Festus (the second governor), and King Herod Agrippa (great-grandson of the Herod who had killed all the baby boys in Bethlehem). None of them convert, but they all listen to Paul with some amount of respect.

Paul held in Rome. God had encouraged Paul that he would one day reach the Romans, and now he has his chance. In 61AD, he is taken by ship to the city of Rome. He is still a prisoner but has moderate freedom on house arrest.

Roman Emperor Nero, persecutor of Jews and Christians

In Rome, Paul is permitted to teach. He spends two years discipling the fledgling church there with very good results. The Book of Acts ends Paul's story at this point, probably because Luke had been with Paul in Caesarea and finished writing it as Paul was awaiting trial in Rome.

From Romans 15:28 we know Paul had been planning a fourth missionary journey to Spain. Some early traditions hold that he got to go somehow. Extra-Biblical history records that Paul was beheaded in Rome under Nero around 67AD. By that point, the Greco-Roman world had a number of very powerful Christian churches, planted in some of the most important cities of that era.

OTHER DISCIPLES

A lot of the New Testament is written by Paul, probably because God's purpose in the New Testament was for the gospel to extend beyond Jerusalem and go into the whole world—and Paul's life represented that task. But other disciples also did amazing work, and the Bible contains epistles written by some of them, including Peter, James, and John.

Importantly, we cannot be certain about the history of Jesus' apostles outside of the New Testament. Extra-Biblical traditions tell many stories, but we do not know for sure what is fact and what is fiction. Here are some things we do know:

Peter. Peter leads the first Christian revival occurring just after Jesus' death (Acts 2). His sermon on the day of Pentecost ushers in 3000 more believers, notably from different cultures because they hear the gospel being preached in their own languages.

Peter and John heal a beggar which leads to another revival of approximately 2000 more believers. Later, Peter will raise a woman from the dead. They perform many healings while the number of disciples keeps growing, so the Roman authorities imprison them. But the Lord sends an earthquake which allows them to escape after only one night. Later, Peter and John are imprisoned again, but Gamaliel's exhortation gets them off with just a flogging (Acts 5).

Peter plays a big part in getting the very first Gentiles saved and into the Church. God sends him a heavenly vision that Cornelius, a Gentile, is going to get saved and usher in a Greek revival. Peter goes to Cornelius and inaugurates the salvation and baptism of his entire household.

At some point, Peter is confronted by Paul about his weak conscience concerning whether the Gentiles ought to keep some of the Jewish laws, especially circumcision (Gal. 2:11-13). Yet, Peter plants the first Gentile church at Antioch and for the rest of his life is a faithful steward of the gospel going out into the world.

After Paul is executed, Peter writes two epistles (1 and 2 Peter) to churches in Asia Minor that Paul planted. He writes them from Rome and remains there until his own execution. Tradition holds that Peter and Paul died in very cruel ways after Nero blamed Christians for the burning of Rome in 64AD—generally believed to have been set by Nero himself.

John. The apostle John spends his early ministry with Peter, preaching in Jerusalem. He witnesses the revival at Pentecost and is imprisoned for preaching and doing miracles along with Peter.

But John outlives the other original apostles. He is not martyred as they are. Tradition holds that he took care of Jesus' mother Mary until her death. Then after the Jewish Temple is destroyed in 70AD, he moves to Ephesus.

It is in Ephesus that he writes his gospel (the Gospel of John) and three epistles (1, 2, and 3 John). This may explain the reflective and love-focused aspect that is unique to John's writing. John likely would have looked back on his time with Jesus as young man, through a much older man's eyes.

While in Greece, John disciples men including Polycarp, Papias, and Ignatius, who become bishops and some of the earliest Church Fathers. This is important because we still have writings from all three of these men. They form an important connecting link between the days of the original apostles and the Early Church.

Ignatius, for example, becomes one of the leaders of the church at Smyrna, which is lovingly addressed in the book of Revelation and also well-attested to in extra-biblical history.

Saint Ignatius

Polycarp was a famous martyr also from Smyrna. With Ignatius, he helps disciple the next generation of Church Fathers who further develop Christian doctrine.

Around 95AD, a new Roman emperor tries to rid Rome of Jews and Christians. John is banished to the island of Patmos where he writes the Book of Revelation. The dates assigned to all of John's writings are generally considered to be between 85-95AD, with Revelation closing the New Testament canon of divine inspiration.

Polycarp, John's disciple

Near the turn of the first century, Christianity was flourishing underground in the Roman empire, but the blending of Christianity and Greco-Roman philosophy was beginning. A whole generation after Jesus' death, many people were trying to make sense of all that had occurred earlier.

John therefore begins the tradition, carried on by subsequent Church Fathers, of writing to correct these heresies. Some scholars say this is why John's writing is the most philosophical, with very unique aspects of Jesus being described (i.e. Jesus as the eternal *Logos* that orders the creation). Joh is therefore sometimes looked to as the first Christian **apologist**, or defender of the faith.

James. The story of James is confusing because there are three James' in the New Testament: 1) James the brother of John, 2) James the son of Alphaeus, and 3) James the Lord's brother. The book of James is commonly regarded to be written by James the Lord's brother.

At first James did not believe Jesus was the Messiah (John 7:2-5), but he eventually believes and becomes an overseer of the Church in Judea (Acts 12:17, Gal. 1:19). James encourages Peter and Paul, and concentrates his own ministry on the Jews in southern Israel. Tradition holds that James was martyred at the Temple in front of the Sanhedrin, and that his epistle was one of the earliest ones written.

Mark. Mark, or "John Mark" as he is referred to in the Scriptures, wrote the Gospel of Mark. He also travelled with the other apostles, including Paul. He goes with Paul on his first missionary journey to Galatia but gets in trouble when he drops out half way through (Acts 13:13). The cousin of Barnabas, he gets adopted onto one of Barnabas' other missions.

Mark eventually reconciles with Paul and appears with him in Rome (Col. 4:10). Then he is specifically asked for, by Paul, to come to Rome while Paul is imprisoned there (2 Tim. 4:11). In between, Mark primarily works with Peter. He goes with Peter to Rome and is commonly said to have based the Gospel of Mark on Peter's recounting everything he remembered Jesus teaching and doing.

Chapter 10:
New Testament Themes

"But when the perfect comes..." (1 Cor. 13:10)

There are so many great foundational messages in the New Testament that it seems almost foolish to try to capture them in a chapter. But the following are just a few keys which contextualize the ministries of Jesus and Paul, and help you unlock greater meaning from the text.

THE END OF THE OLD COVENANT

At the time of Jesus' birth, the Jews were looking for deliverance from their king and empire. They saw the Romans as pagan oppressors who backed their king, Herod, and made him a compromiser. In the days of the Prophets, God had promised that a Son of David would arise to restore Israel's kingdom, and that that kingdom would reign forever. But the Jews knew they could never be what God had called them to be while under the rulership of the Gentiles.

Over the years, men in Judea had arisen to lead a revolt with this motivation. The Romans had to put down each one. Jesus will appear to fit this pattern, and that is how the Jews will convince the Romans to order His execution.

When Jesus comes, He is not the Messiah the Jews are expecting. Instead of restoring the kingdom to Israel through conquest and kingly authority, He wanders about doing miracles, healings, and sermons on mountains. He is modest and low key—very anti-climactic.

Additionally, Jesus doesn't congratulate the Jewish leadership for guarding the faith—He condemns them! He reinterprets the Scriptures they thought they knew so well, and probes their hearts to see if they are really hungry for God.

Only some have eyes to see and ears to hear what is really going on. The Jews' history and circumstances had conditioned them to look for the reestablishment of the physical Kingdom of Israel, complete with the old covenants, laws, and promises. But God had something much grander in His mind – a new covenant, a final covenant, which would eclipse all the others.

Though many did not see it at the time, God had promised this new covenant through the Prophets. For example, Jeremiah prophesied:

> "Behold, **days are coming**," declares the Lord, "when I will make **a new covenant** with the house of Israel and with the house of Judah, **not like** the covenant which I made with their fathers in the day I took them by the hand to bring them out of the land of Egypt, My covenant which they broke, although I was a husband to them," declares the Lord.

> "But this is the covenant which I will make with the house of Israel after those days," declares the Lord, "I will put My law **within** them and **on their heart** I will write it; and I will be their God, and they shall be My people. They will not teach again, each man his neighbor and each man his brother, saying, 'Know the Lord,' for they will all know Me, from the least of them to the greatest of them," declares the Lord, "for I will **forgive** their iniquity, and **their sin I will remember no more**." (Jeremiah 31:31-34)

The Prophets foretold the New Covenant which would be made in Jesus' blood, but it was veiled. When Jesus preaches this new covenant, most can't understand it—they keep asking Him when He will restore the old kingdom. Even His disciples expect it.

Jesus instead preaches that mankind is being redeemed by a God who loves them. He says they will have fellowship with Him on earth and be with Him in heaven if they follow and walk as He walks. He says they must have faith like a child, avoid the temptations of this life, and eat His body and drink His blood if they want to be His disciples. The general response from everyone is that this is very hard to accept.

Jesus also challenges Jewish leadership on what being a good Jew means—not staying at home on the Sabbath but doing the works of God; not starving the sheep but giving them the nourishment they need; not laying on burdensome regulations but lifting them off. He tells them that their ancestry is of no importance to God, and that when He dies, the Temple will pass away and all the Law will be fulfilled.

This goes against the prevailing interpretation of the Old Testament, and the leaders can't accept it. They have become so spiritually blind through their traditions and ancestry that they call for Jesus' execution. The Sanhedrin convicts Him and get the Romans to do the dirty work.

THE NEW ISRAEL

Jesus' crucifixion cements the fate of the nation Israel. They try, convict, and reject Jesus, God Himself in the flesh—their own God who has nurtured them all this time. They even team up with the pagan system they purportedly hate, to get rid of Him.

Probably for the sake of the saints within Israel, God gives the nation a grace period of another 40 years after Jesus' death to repent before it is destroyed by the Roman authorities.

Meanwhile, the early apostles preach fervently in Jewish synagogues to gather whatever remnant of believing Israel is left— the books of James, Hebrews, and Acts all testify to this. Then the Temple in Jerusalem is desecrated and burned in 70 AD by an extremely cruel Roman emperor. Probation is over. Old Israel is gone.

Just as in the Old Testament days, God permits Israel's pagan enemies to conquer them and send them into exile. This time, Jews are scattered all over the world, in exile for almost 2000 years. Jerusalem, Jesus said, would be trampled by Gentiles until the New Covenant worked its way into all of the peoples of the world (Luke 21:24). New Israel has begun.

It is important to see the story of Old Israel and New Israel as one story. The story of Israel climaxes and is completed in the New Testament—it doesn't end with the Old. In fact, the name "Israel" which was originally given to the patriarch Jacob, means "will struggle/rule with God." Most of the "struggle" is described in the Old Testament, and reaches its climax during Jesus' ministry.

Then the story turns. It claims its "rule" with God as sin is conquered and the gospel goes to free the captives across the world. Complete rulership is the prophetic destination at the End of history; all struggle will be over.

In other words, the story of Israel, God's chosen people, comes to fruition in the gospels when the Jewish government and priesthood rejects Jesus' covenant. This covenant in His blood is given to the Gentile church, which becomes a second or substitute son. This new son will not reproduce heirs naturally, but they will spiritually—by "adoption" into His Kingdom (Romans 8:15). Jesus explains this in His parables, notably the Prodigal Son and the Wedding Feast.

Throughout the rest of the New Testament, however, Old Israel grapples with the proclamation of the gospel and new covenant. Jesus disturbs their theology, and then the apostles disturb it even more, especially Paul. They can't accept or figure out why God would change His focus from them to the godless people they had been fighting their entire history?

Old Israel had lost sight of the fact that this had been God's plan all along (Galatians 3:8). God had made *universal* covenants with Adam and Noah. Abraham was given the promise to bless the *entire* globe, "all nations on earth," (Gen. 12:3) before he was circumcised or there was an Israel. Abraham was not just promised to be the father of God's chosen people, but the father of *many* nations. Israel was just a step in that plan to bless, or leaven, the world.

In contrast, God made *national* covenants with Isaac, Jacob, Moses, Joshua, and David. These were about enlarging and prospering Israel as a kingdom or empire. But even under national Israel, their mission was still to be a light to all nations. Their blessing was contingent upon them influencing other people groups, not the other way around.

FROM EXTERNAL TO INTERNAL

God had spoken through the Prophets and old covenants about what He was going to do through Jesus for the world. When Jesus finally came, He fulfilled these prophecies by offering redemption to anyone who would accept Him. His new terms were that eternal life belonged to all who believed in Him but eternal judgment was for all who rejected Him.

There were eternal consequences at stake now, for being obedient—not just health, wealth, or earthly benefits. Jesus and the apostles made it clear that there was not going to be another chance for people to repent and come to God—this was it. The host of the wedding feast was going to close the door, and whomever was still outside was going to miss the marriage banquet.

The Church is the heir of this baton pass. The Church is the new Israel, the new chosen people, the new nation of God. You are the new Kingdom.

We hear so much about "the Kingdom of God" that it can be hard to appreciate the term. God once had a real kingdom in Israel—a physical kingdom that was the envy of the nations. But that kingdom turned on Him so He *went back* to the globe—the people groups who had rejected Him of old—to create another, bigger kingdom that would never pass away.

The gospel that you are preaching now, with all the teachings of Jesus and the apostles, are the new instructions for this Kingdom. The New Testament is the new "constitution" which explains how God's new "nation" will govern itself.

When you read and act on the New Testament you are displacing the old kingdom and enlarging the new one. You are confronting "the kingdoms of this world" that Satan offered Jesus but had no authority to keep. You encounter pagan kingdoms and false religious ideas, and help supplant them. This is bringing God's kingdom from heaven to earth. It is fulfilling the Great Commission.

This is why Paul is so emphatic that if anyone preaches any other gospel—any *other* kind of kingdom—they are accursed (Galatians 1:8-9). They are preaching the things God has judged and will destroy, and enlarging the pool of people who will be condemned with them.

> And Jesus said to them, "**Earnestly have I longed** to eat this Passover meal with you before I suffer..." (Luke 22:15)

The Bible is the story of God longing to redeem man so He can come and dwell with him again. With Jesus' sacrifice, the last rung on the ladder of redemption is finally complete. God has come to live inside of the heart of man, to take up His place on the earth. He no longer needs a physical temple to dwell where man can visit Him— He now dwells among and inside His people. As He fellowships with them personally, the whole earth can be filled with His glory as the waters cover the sea.

Righteousness is no longer based on externalities like good works or animal sacrifices but on the atoning blood of Jesus, the perfect sacrifice. The Law, with its complex stipulations, has been fulfilled by Jesus since He was perfectly obedient and passed all the tests Israel (and we) could not. God's purposes are no longer limited to a single people and their religious and civil ordinances. The Kingdom is leavening itself inside of the national cultures of every people in the world.

Therefore the choice is no longer, "Are you a part of national Israel, with its rules and regulations?" but, "Are you a part of *spiritual* Israel, ruling your heart through the Spirit of God?" It is no longer, "Do you follow the Law God gave to Moses?" but, "Is the Law of God written on your heart? Do you follow it?" His sheep hear His voice and another voice they do not follow.

The Kingdom has moved from external to internal. The tablets of stone, given to man who had a heart of stone, have been replaced with the Spirit, and given to man with a heart of flesh. God promised this in the Old Testament (Jer. 31:33), and He fulfilled it in the New (2 Cor. 3:3).

The new covenant doesn't "spiritualize" these concepts, it makes them a reality. It makes possible all the inward realities of the old covenants by abolishing the external rules they were bound up under (Gal. 3:23). They were abolished in Jesus' flesh when God's enmity with man disappeared (Eph. 2:15).

This means that the New Testament does not delete the Old Testament, as some scholars have argued. Rather, it fulfills it. It expands it. It's important to understand this so you yourself can build off the Old Testament rather than delete it. If you obsolete the realities of the old concepts, like priesthood and circumcision, you miss a huge part of your identity as a Christian. God has the same vision for you that He had for Israel back then—to be priests and kings that walk humbly with our God—you just aren't living under the Law to obtain it!

You are living under grace to obtain it. You are not commanded to choose God, or walk in His ways, but you choose to. God doesn't give you the Law and its regulations, but He gives you His Son and His model—a freer but much higher standard. You get the freedom of not living in works, but you also get the responsibility of circumcising your own heart. We don't have to worry that we broke a rule or commandment, but we do have to worry about being lukewarm.

In other words, grace is a better and harder covenant to live under. We are free but are supposed to use our freedom for Jesus. This is what God has wanted since Adam and Eve, in the Garden. You could say that that is what made the Garden, truly Paradise.

If this is the difficult part of the gospel, the fact is that there is a great reward. The New Covenant fulfilled everything God had been working for since the Fall. Satan, the evil serpent, was crushed at the Cross, along with his authority to rule the world. This was stripped away and given back to a man, Jesus, the last Adam.

Not only did Jesus fulfill the covenants, but He was a different kind of man—a *new creation*, with a new nature. By faith, we live in and experience this new creation (2 Cor. 5:17). The death that reigned in the creation Adam ruined through sin, is being replaced by the life that reigns through Christ and His eternal life (Rom. 5:17). This is an ever-expanding Kingdom that has no end (Isaiah 9:7).

The remainder of history is the filling and replacing of the old with the new. Jesus said, "All authority in heaven and earth has been given to me" (Matt. 28:18). This is the restoration of everything Adam had in the Garden, including authority over the serpent. Jesus endured the baptism of fire from Eden's flaming sword, and crossed from the outer wilderness back into the Garden of perfect fellowship with the Father. We do this in Him. A greater reality could hardly be imagined.

LIVING IN THE NEW COVENANT NOW

Jesus obtained the promises of old covenants and gives us greater ones. He restores us to the relationship with God we were meant to have. Now you can walk and talk with God as Adam did, even though you don't yet see Him face to face.

You can do this because God has made peace with you by forgiving your sins. Anyone can be saved, even the lowliest of sinners as Paul called himself, because God's wrath towards sin is satisfied. You can stand confidently before God because He feels merciful towards you when you repent. Jesus' punishment in your place lets you come boldly before the throne of grace.

No other people in the past had this blessing. Most were afraid of God. But Jesus draws you near to God. Jesus reveals God as He was originally, as "Abba Father." In the Old Testament, very few experienced God as their Father. When you were born again, you were placed into the family of God as an adopted son. The whole Church, by extension, has been adopted as His children, co-heirs with Him (Rom. 8:17).

As children and co-heirs, you have more authority than people had under the previous covenants. Some in the Old Testament experienced the power of the Holy Spirit, but now everyone who is in Christ can. Jesus' Name is the basis of this power. Jesus gives you the authority to take back what the devil stole. You are promised that as His representative, the gates of hell cannot prevail against you. You are His hands and feet, with authority to preach, teach, heal, and restore. Your own mouth is now the vessel for eternal life. This is an amazing delegation of power.

While some godly men in the Old Testament knew forgiveness and justification by faith, few experienced the glory and power of walking in the Holy Spirit. Only a few forerunners like Elijah and Elisha demonstrated what a life full of God could look like. But the New Testament insists that Elijah was a man just like us (James 5:17). The New Testament brings all believers into the fullness of the glory of God, promising us comfort, victory, the mind of Christ, and the prompting of the Spirit.

In Jesus, unity based on God instead of sin has also become real. When the Holy Spirit was poured out at Pentecost, hearers spoke in other tongues and the wall of hostility which God put between nations at Babel was torn down. This means we can experience the glory of the new covenant ourselves, but also corporately. Together, this glory can go to an even greater dimension.

You can participate in His glory every day if you set your heart to do it. We see through a glass dimly, but the universal invitation to partake in God's glory is an astounding distinctive of the gospel. Instead of some saints in older times having some blessings some of the time, God has satisfied all the requirements for you to have it any time, all the time. The results are now up to you.

Chapter 11:
His Kingdom Coming

What do we do now that Jesus has come? Or put another way, what do we do now that He is gone? Is the Church just waiting for the End Times? Are we preaching the gospel to whomever we can before the Rapture occurs?

The Book of Revelation is confusing for many, so it's easy to have questions in these areas. While the study of God's Kingdom and the End Times is an area where many questions cannot be fully answered, we do know that Jesus appears victorious, and us with Him in the End. In heaven there is victory, and eventually on earth there will be.

The important thing is to realize that He told us these things to encourage us—not scare or confuse us. He wants us to live in the awareness that His foot is about to crush the head of the serpent. Then the gap between His perfect promises and the fallen world that rebels against them will disappear.

CONTINUITY

God has not changed since the time of the Bible's authorship. God's character and plan have not changed since mankind began. He has always wanted to redeem us, and each covenant He made led man further up the redemptive ladder.

This means the age we're living in now follows the same trajectory as the times that came before – God reaching out to mankind in ever expanding ways. Although there will not be another covenant coming, we're still living in Jesus' covenant now. It isn't over.

It isn't even over just because the New Testament is closed. The things Jesus set in motion are still growing in scope throughout the world. We're the instruments of that happening. We're the instruments of the same new covenant He set in motion 2000 years ago.

Therefore, a proper view of the world today should emphasize *continuity* and *connection* with the time of the Scripture. Just as it is wrong to see a huge gap in God's purposes between the Old and New Testaments, it is wrong to see a huge gap in God's purposes between the time of the Bible and the time of today.

Unfortunately, many people have been influenced by a theology called **dispensationalism** which emphasizes *discontinuity* in the phases of history. Dispensationalism says God deals with mankind in very separate stages: God had one method of redemption during Abraham, another during Moses, another during Jesus, and another now. He will eventually have a different one in the future. Instead of viewing history as a unified whole, dispensationalists divide both Bible history and Church history into different phases with different operating principles. Nowhere is this more controversial than in teachings about God's coming Kingdom and the End Times.

The End Times

It is popular among dispensationalists to teach that the End Times is a future period of time with its own special principles and schedule of events that separates it from all other phases of history. In one common End Times scenario, the Church will be raptured out in the beginning of a sequence of horrible events. This makes believers an apprehensive group of people waiting around for it. After the Rapture, God will then get around to finishing up the rest of history the way He really wanted to—with a restored physical kingdom of Israel, kings and priests, a new Temple, etc.

In this view, the Body of Christ is seen as an interesting parenthetical in history, not part of God's ever-advancing plan. It is a piece to be done away with, not what he was getting around to the whole time.

For most of the 20th century, and even today, a growing segment of the Church has gotten caught up in dispensationalism and thinking about how the End Times will unfold, instead of the mission in the meantime. We are taught that our culture is going to the devil and we must just do our best as things get worse and worse.

This leads people to think of the Church as a group of suffering saints, gloomy and ineffective. The hope is that Jesus will appear soon and rapture the Church out of the mess on earth. This perspective has caused the majority of evangelical Christians to hold a dismal view of the Church's ability to succeed in a lost and dying world, and therefore discouraged to try. Evangelism is relegated to saving people—praying the prayer—as fast as possible before the sinking ship goes down. Once the very last person in the very last tribe on earth has heard the good news from a missionary, the heavens will open and Jesus will descend.

Some have inserted an additional End Times revival as part of the sequence of events to make things appear more positive. When the signs of final tribulation and apostasy start to show, we can get really excited because we know "real" revival like no-one has ever seen before will overtake the earth. Jews and other nations which have been spiritually blind up until now will suddenly flock to Jesus because God will cause it to happen.

But this implies that all generations prior to this last generation are of less consequence. Our actions are weak in comparison to God's. If this were true, the main event after getting born-again would be Jesus' return. The most important part of beginning a journey with Him would be the end of it!

Jesus Himself warned us against this futile thinking (Matt. 24:23-36). End Times scenarios are guesswork that very few will ever see play out, and they distract the Church from its mission to proclaim the gospel, disciple the nations, and purify itself.

Moreover, this whole approach fundamentally misunder-stands what the Church was assigned to do and has been doing for most of its 2000 years. Christian civilization has not been huddled under a rock hoping desperately for the End. The Church has sent martyrs to die, missionaries to evangelize, scholars to the printing presses, and ambassadors to culture. It has been obeying the Great Commission to teach all nations to obey and follow Christ.

What about you? The New Testament was given to you as a guide to take part in this incredibly great task. This is how you should read the Book of Revelation and how you should think of yourself in God's historical plan.

THE LAST DAYS

But couldn't the End could come at any minute? Well, why do we think the End is so imminent? Because things are bad? Maybe they are so bad because we're think the End is so imminent!

You can see the catch-22. Many Christians insist we are living the Last Days before Jesus' return because of the amount opposition the Church faces... but we're facing opposition because we've been assuming it's the End. In American culture, we have largely laid down in front of opposition because we have accepted it as a sign of the times. Then we retreat or get persecuted out of the spheres of influence we once had. This begs the question: what if we didn't assume it was the End—how would we act then?

It's not just a rhetorical question. Many don't realize that the New Testament teaches that the Last Days is not a future event—it is a continuous event that has been going on since Jesus defeated Satan at the Cross. The entire period from Christ until His return is the Last Days (Heb. 1:2).

How can this be? The Last Days are described as a period of corruption and signs that you actually see in every generation. When you study church history you see that opposition isn't new—the Church has always faced opposition, but it wasn't a sign of the End. In fact, it was often a sign of the beginning!

Facing opposition is what the Church does. You can't view opposition as a sign that we're near the End, or that it's ok to give up. The gospel does not go forth without opposition. We're supposed to be busy bringing in the End goal—the Great Commission—not watching and waiting, and assuming our time will run out any moment. We aren't saving a few to get them in the boat before the ship goes down. We are strategically building for the future as if there is a future.

If this is a new way of thinking for you, consider that many of the greatest things Christians have accomplished in contemporary culture, such as traction in the pro-life movement, have been gained when Christians have assumed future generations were coming and large-scale changes needed to be made for their sakes. Good Christian witness requires optimistic, long-term thinkers with intelligence, business management skills, political interest, and other skills. It is hard to build these up when you think the End might occur tonight.

WHAT DOES REVELATION SAY?

Of course the world will end someday, and we are always one day closer! But the Book of Revelation tells us that for as long as the Church Age exists, we are in the middle of a spiritual war caused by the Great Commission. The devil is trying to build his kingdom, Babylon, which is proud of its idolatry and wrath against the saints. God is building His Kingdom which will ultimately triumph.

In Revelation, this war plays out. We see the City of God in all its splendor, and that it conquers the City of Man. But for a brief moment, the idolatrous city seems like it will win. It murders the

Church, grins over its adultery, and rides the full-grown beast of Satan.

But then we catch a glimpse of Jesus in all *His* splendor, gleaming and powerful. He fulfills God's promises by crushing evil in the winepress, reclaiming the Tree of Life for us, wiping away every tear, and healing the nations. We're allowed to see the story as God sees it, which is a championing of His will, through His own Son.

We're commonly taught, however, to see Revelation as a book about the future instead of a book about the present. Of course it has future fulfillment, when the End of history comes and Jesus returns. But It is not just apocalyptic literature about End Times events. It is a description of the timeless spiritual war between good and evil. It has relevance to every generation that will read it, not just the last one before Jesus' return.

God did not give Revelation or any other part of the Bible so you would speculate about times, dates, and seasons in the future. He gave it to all people at all times to encourage them while they were on the mission. He wanted them to know the forces they were up against and how they operate—but also how they will not win. Rather than read Revelation as a code book for special secrets that will occur before Jesus comes again, you should read it as a series of patterns that will be seen in every church generation's lifetime.

Consider how Revelation opens, with the admonitions to the seven churches. There was a past application of these prophecies to the real seven churches in the Greek world. There are ongoing applications of them to our churches today. There will also be an End Times fulfillment of those exhortations. This is sometimes called **recapitulation,** or multiple fulfillments. Whatever the Bible tells historically has relevance for all eras because the same patterns repeat. Or put a different way, as history moves in cycles, Scripture from the past becomes relevant to the present and the future.

Consider the Antichrist. Many people are worried about the End Times Antichrist, but John teaches us that there are "many antichrists" (1 John 2:18). There is not just a single, final person who will oppose God—there are many people who have opposed God all throughout history: Pharaoh, Caesar, Nero, Mohammad, Hitler, Stalin... They are all antichrists, and there will be more to come.

There will also be a final Apostasy, but there have already been apostasies in every generation. There will be a final Tribulation, but even today there are tribulations—earthquakes, famines, signs of the end. Jesus specifically warns us when we see these things, "do not say the end is near" because they are just birth pangs. Every generation will have them until the End comes because the City of Man and the City of God are growing, head to head, tares to wheat. The devil's kingdom gets larger and larger, but so does God's. As they conflict, the scale of opposition increases. History repeats itself as the devil gears up for his final showdown with God.

But continuity is the key. The events at the End will be more similar to what we have seen on earth, than they will be different. The same forces which oppose God's Kingdom in the beginning keep opposing it over and over again, all the way until a final opposition at the End of history.

Many have been confused on this account because of a misreading of Revelation and assumption that it is only about a timeline of future events instead of devotional in nature and applicable to us today. This is indeed the purpose of the entire Bible—to encourage believers in every generation to understand the times and know what to do. God told us where it all started in Genesis and where it was all going in Revelation so that anyone born at any time could pick up the Bible and have the right framework for their place in the mission.

How do we discern the right framework for this mission? It starts with the biggest picture. Hebrews 9:17 explains that salvation is a two-stage process because there are two comings of Christ. When Jesus came to earth the first time, He defeated Satan and broke the chains of death. Through faith in this act of Jesus, we are now "saved"—both now and for the future.

The first part of salvation is the part we understand most. Jesus' first coming broke God into creation and established a beachhead for His Kingdom to spread the way He always wanted.

But the second part is less certain. At the end of history, when the Church has completed its mission to disciple all the nations, Jesus will return and consummate His victory. Sin and death will finally bow, Satan will be utterly destroyed, and people will all be resurrected in body to either live with Him forever in a new heavens and earth, or live apart from Him forever in hell.

The Church Age is what lies in between these two comings. It is the period of the outworking of Christ's victory. The Bible calls this period *the Last Days* (or sometimes, "latter days"). It is the last period of history where the Church preaches the gospel, disciples the nations, and purifies itself so God's Kingdom will spread.

God's Kingdom is wherever God is King! It is not a location, but an invisible reality where His will is being expressed, He has dominion over opposing entities, and His fruit is being seen. When two or three gather in His name, the Kingdom is there. Where peace and love permeate, the Kingdom is there. When people repent and do good to one another instead, the Kingdom is there. God's ways coming to the earth to supplant the devil's is His Kingdom.

This has been established already, through Jesus' first coming, but it is not yet fully completed. It must spread over the entire world and create a people who reflect God's image the way He intended through Adam.

God says this time will be extremely fruitful, like a tree whose branches fill the air, or a mountain that spreads and takes over the whole earth. The Church Age is an era of planting and growth which, when Jesus returns, will end with a great harvest.

Because we are living in this in-between stage, we experience a tension between what Jesus has legally done for us and what actually manifests on earth. We are in the process of walking out what Jesus has promised, over the Fall. Some theologians have called this the "*already but not yet*" aspect of the Kingdom.

The New Testament promotes this worldview. Jesus was the firstfruits of what God wanted to do on the earth—the firstborn from the dead (1 Cor. 15:20). But you and I will not be raised from the dead or receive our glorified body until He comes again. We've been born-again but there is both a "now" and a "prophetic" aspect to this reality.

We've been called to live in this "already but not yet" state in many aspects of living for God, not just being born again. We know what the divine promises are but can't actualize them perfectly. People still get sick, they die or suffer. We want the radiant glory of God to show up and do what it has promised to do! We want the healing, the miracles, the love and restoration He has promised. We want it corporately, in our worship, in our services, and in our Christian community... now! We are called to hope and usher in this hope.

But we are all collectively walking out the Judgment on sin that Jesus enacted. It will end when the End comes, but meanwhile, we walk it out in relationship with God. So God's Kingdom is here now but is also still to come. His children are walking out its establishment in greater and greater measure.

Living in this tension can be hard on our hearts at times, but there is a great benefit. The Church Age, or Last Days, is synonymous with the time when the message of salvation is being proclaimed to the whole world... and people are accepting every day! They are escaping judgment to come and starting a life-giving walk with Him now. One day, God will decide to complete or close this offer, and then there will be no more chance to be reconciled to God. We shouldn't wish this to be over any sooner than it has to be.

THY KINGDOM COME

While we're here, the Church's mission is nothing less than to bring heaven to earth. This is what Jesus taught His disciples to pray— your Kingdom come on earth as it is in heaven (Matt. 6:10). The rule, character, and most importantly, the presence of God is being brought to the earth through the Church.

Although this has dramatic implications for life on earth, the focus is not on setting up a new physical kingdom like the nation of Israel. The focus is on God's people leavening every nation and culture and changing them from within.

In that sense, the Church is a secret invasion of the entire world system. Wherever it goes, the world will be at war with it but nothing will be able to stop it. Satan has already been defeated and authority has been transferred to Jesus. What remains in the rest of history is for us to exercise that authority and remove Satan from power wherever he may be found.

This doesn't mean we're building a utopia or theocracy. We're seasoning, salting, and reforming civilization so God's character can be seen. This can be done with the same kindness and gentleness that Jesus Himself showed when He encountered the lost.

This challenges the End Times idea that God's kingdom will be set up again on earth physically, either before or after Jesus comes again. Although God's Kingdom, as prophesied in Daniel 2, will shake and destroy empires and kingdoms, it is not itself a governmental entity. It is an invisible community of believers who are ruling and reigning with Him now from heaven. It is the family God sought from the beginning—His Body, in which He dwells.

When we spread His rule, we bring wholeness of every kind: love, mercy, kindness, unity, healing, and provision. In contrast to other systems, which have tried to take dominion through war or tyranny, God's "conquering" message is that He is at peace with the world! He told Paul that *forgiveness* would open people's eyes and cause them to "turn from the dominion of Satan to God" (Acts 28:18). Jesus is the "hope of the world," the dove after the Flood who brings His message to the whole world that wrath is over.

Traditionally, spreading the Kingdom of God has been seen mostly as preaching the gospel unto conversion. Jesus certainly did commission us to go into the world and preach the good news to every living creature, baptizing them in the Lord's name (Mt. 28:18-20). But the Great Commission was not new. It was a restatement of the commission originally given to both Adam and Noah—to fill the earth and take dominion over it—except requiring conversion and baptism because the world is fallen and needs cleansing.

When you put both commissions side by side, you see they are bookends to one another. They require each other for God's will to be fulfilled on the earth. That is not conversion only. It is conversion unto a purpose. The original commission to "fill the earth and take dominion" is supposed to be fulfilled through Jesus' commission as we preach the good news and baptize.

It is through proclaiming Jesus's atonement for sin that God's dominion will spread through the earth. All things have been made by Him and for Him, and it is to Him that all things in rebellion will eventually bow. It is not through our own force or coercion.

The result of preaching the gospel is therefore more than just souls converted, bound for heaven. It is profound impact on the way life is actually lived on earth. Most Christians hear the Great Commission to mean "make disciples from out of all nations," but the original Greek should be translated more directly, like going to "disciple the nations." "Discipling" means bringing God's order, His ways, His blessings, to all nations—not just rescuing souls out of them. It includes things like abolishing slavery, bringing political peace, restoring families, etc.

Rescuing some is just the start of what is possible in God as the history of the early church in Rome shows. In Chapter 2, we saw how first the followers of God were few and mightily persecuted. Then Christianity grew to such an extent that it took over the Roman Empire. The leaders converted and discipled unbelievers under their jurisdiction, prohibiting Zeus worship, gladiatorial games, indecent sexuality, and all the pagan practices of Rome. While the history of imperial Christianity gets a bad rap today, it is hard to overestimate the amount of "discipling the nations" it accomplished. It made the ancient world completely disappear.

Since that time, the Church has led the way for democracy, free market economies, modern science, and humanitarianism to prosper the world—just from building on Biblical principles. These institutions witness His character and ensure a safe place for God's people to dwell. They show God's love and mercy towards all people, even those who hate Him.

Additionally, the modern world Christianity has built—with separation of church and state, freedom of speech, etc.—ensures that the Church can continue on its Great Commission. In the Early Church era, this was extremely difficult. If future generations of Christians hadn't bravely faced the systems opposing them, God's people would still be persecuted in most places, and missions would be much more difficult.

In other words, discipling nations and transforming society goes hand in hand with spreading the gospel and spiritual revival; they aren't two separate spheres. A discipled nation has culturally engaged Christians, which results in a base for further evangelism. A discipled nation also achieves political freedom and wealth, which can make missions wider and more successful, as you see in the cases of Reinhardt Bonnke, Heidi Baker, and others. It's not that wealth and freedom are required of Christianity, but they can be good wingmen. Because of those things, we can be the seat of missions and charity today for the whole world. Likewise, good Christian principles make effective people and systems who want more of it.

THE CHURCH AS GOD'S VESSEL

The goal of proclaiming the gospel and discipling the nations is the symbolic return to Eden—the tabernacling of God among His people to the point where His presence covers the whole earth "as the waters cover the sea." The altar, the Tabernacle, and the Temple were all forerunners of the Church. They were shadows of the true and heavenly sanctuary which God wanted to build in man.

God gave instructions for these buildings and showed His presence "within the veil" or the Holy of Holies. But this was always supposed to foreshadow His presence in our hearts, the most sacred place there is. When our hearts assemble together in our churches and communities, we become the temple of the living God. A successful church can resemble Eden, even before we are finally taken there.

There are of course naysayers of the Church, just as there have been throughout history. The institutional church is not perfect. There have been many things it has needed to correct over the centuries. But it is has been the most prominent reforming vessel on earth so far—the basis of revival, social reform, teaching, counseling, and change. It has also been a base, refuge, and springboard for Christian activity—more than individuals in isolation.

God has been in the process of purifying and reforming His Church since its inception. It has been correcting heresy, putting out false teachers, creating new doctrine, and experimenting with leadership models. This really took off during the days of the Protestant Reformers, who yearned to recreate the New Testament church. They did much to restore the Church to the Bible and the Holy Spirit.

Contemporary Christians have followed suit. The result of hundreds of years of refinement and testing is that the Bible-believing church is closer to the original New Testament church than ever before. There is scorn heaped upon it, but God is moving the Church from glory to glory. Even if you just compare one aspect of church today, like worship, to what it was like twenty years ago, or forty years ago, there is no comparison. The Church is purifying itself and coming into its fullness. This includes its ability to love.

People pronouncing God's judgment against the Church are therefore in the wrong spirit. The Church is His Body, what He sent His Son to die for, which the gates of hell will not prevail against. Including the history of Israel, the global Church today is thousands of years in the making. It began in God's heart during the counsel of the Trinity at Creation, and He launched it the moment Abraham put Isaac on the altar. God Himself came as its capstone, 2000 years later. He then commissioned mere men to take it forward into all the world.

Since that time, the Church has never stopped advancing. And since the time of the Protestant Reformation, it has never stopped becoming more like what God wants it to be.

The end of this great masterwork will be that the Church lives on to experience with God the fulfillment of all of His dreams in eternity. The enemy and evil itself will be defeated forever, and a family of billions of children who love Him will worship around Him for eternity. Paradise will be regained, and this time it will be full— partly because of the good things the Church did and the refuge it was, so believers did not have to live and act in isolation from one another.

CONCLUSION

The Church Age is therefore exciting! It is a time of active mercy. Each day is another chance for someone to come to Christ, and we are part of that. Some of us want the era to be over and God to just end it all, but that overlooks God's real heart and mission to save every tribe, tongue, and people of the earth. This is the mission we have been assigned, and we have been given an authority that Satan cannot thwart.

Do not allow some reading of Revelation to take your eyes off that mission. You're not supposed to be hanging out until the Rapture, or even evangelizing just to stay busy. Revelation tells you your current mission is to confront the powers of this world and despoil Satan's kingdom. Together, you are part of something bigger—the Church bringing His Kingdom from heaven to earth. God is using you to restore and replenish, to call the earth back into His dominion.

This is a much larger, complex plan. What matters is not what final events God has ordained for the future, but your role now in moving toward them.

Waiting for the End and wanting Jesus to come back is not the message of the New Testament. That is cowering at Satan's power and refusing to do God's will. God is a victorious warrior and His army is the Church! There are lost souls to save and as well as marvelous things to do with them after that. The Church Age is an age of people bringing things into their fullness, through Jesus. The Body of Christ suffers as they advance against Satan, but will be rewarded and set free into a new world where it regains the Tree of Life.

The end of the story is that all the saints who died in faith, believing in the One to come, will be resurrected to everlasting joy and righteousness. There will be no more division, pain, or sadness. There will be complete healing of the nations in an everlasting kingdom. Jesus will be the light and we will worship Him forever in thanks for what He's given. That will end God's redemption plan and fulfill all the promises He ever made to mankind. Hallelujah! Come, Lord Jesus!

~ Part III ~
How to Study the Bible

Chapter 12:
Approaching the Text

Have you ever sat in a sermon and wondered, "Wow! How did he get that revelation?" Or had a friend who seems to be able to enjoy the most engrossing times with the Scripture, bringing forth the most fascinating revelations with ease while you struggle to get anything from your devotional time? Perhaps you have even taken a course or two about the Bible only to be more perplexed, and no closer to the goal of knowing God more.

Bible interpretation is a complex subject which could merit a lifetime of study. Although all Bible-believing Christians come to the Bible with a reverence for Scripture and a desire to interpret it rightly, many find themselves, even after years of study, wanting a deeper ability to understand and derive meaning from the Word. This is because we bring assumptions to the Bible when we read it, and some of those hinder revelation.

This section of the book is designed to examine and refine how you approach the Bible so you can have a deeper encounter with God. How you approach it, and the principles you use to interpret, are called **hermeneutics**. Your hermeneutics, whether you have ever studied the subject or not, are incredibly important in determining the results you will get.

HAVING THE RIGHT HEART

Before getting into principles, however, it's important to stress that there is more to Bible interpretation than rules. It is easy to think if you just learn the right rules, you will get the correct interpretation of the Scripture. The problem with this idea is that it neglects the fact that interpretation is necessarily heavily dependent on the interpreter – you.

What you bring to the text in your heart has an immense amount to do with what you will get out of the text. What questions do you have? Why are you reading the Bible? What are you hoping to get out of it? The questions you ask will determine the answers you find. If you read to learn trivia, you will learn trivia. If you read to feel good about yourself, you will get fleeting satisfaction. If you read to confirm your personal theories, you will find confirmation. But if you read to draw near to God, you will draw near to God.

The Bible is the Word of God. It brings a pure perspective from heaven which challenges everything about the way mankind wants things to be. What this means is that the first and most important requirement for interpreting it correctly is that your heart is postured to be changed by what you read.

Only when you are reading the Bible to seriously discover what God wants you to change about your life and heart attitudes, can you hope to properly interpret it.

Foundational to this entire process is whether or not you believe that the Bible is true and the extent to which you believe it. When you encounter a difficult and challenging passage, do you challenge the Bible or do you allow it to challenge you? If you believe that you have direct instructions from God when you read the Bible, and you act on the instructions, you will be changed. But you cannot be changed by something you are not absolutely certain is true.

Another way to say this is, the goal of reading Scripture is application, not information. If your heart is not willing to apply what you read, then reading will be to no avail. It may make you feel good, or provide you some wisdom for our situation, but true intimacy with God will not be achieved.

In order to grow closer to God, you need to meditate on and apply what you read, allowing the Spirit of God to search your heart and test your innermost thoughts. This will not only aid the sanctification process, but it will expand your love and dependence on the Cross.

Jesus frequently exhorted those around Him by saying, "He who has ears to hear, let him hear." He was challenging us to open our spiritual ears to hear what God is saying and be changed by it. Sin in your heart and life therefore has a major impact on your ability to get revelation from the Bible. You obviously will not be able to hear truth about areas you are not willing to change, but at an even deeper level, sin dulls your heart from hearing the Word of God. It clouds your ability to hear God through the text. You feel the Bible is dry or worse. By contrast, when sin is not in the way, your heart is soft and you will naturally draw meaning and life out of God's words. Repentance opens the door to revelation.

GOD OR HIS WORD?

The Bible is the gateway to knowing God. It is not a substitute for knowing Him. The Pharisees made this fatal mistake when they understood the prophecies about Jesus but did not recognize Him when He was there in person. Jesus told them, "You diligently study the Scriptures because you think that by them you possess eternal life. These are the Scriptures that testify about me." (John 5:39). Jesus was telling them the goal of reading the Bible is not to know the Bible—it is to know God.

Contemporary Christian culture is slowly coming to this realization, but it is still a significant source of difficulty for many growing in the faith. Recognizing the amazing potential and importance of God's Word for life, preachers commonly exhort you to read your Bible every day. They press you to "get your quiet time" or "do your devotional." The idea communicated is that by doing these things, you magically become a good Christian.

Part of what is silly about this idea is that for 1600 years of church history, and for some even today, it wasn't even possible for most Christians to have a daily time with the Bible—it hadn't been printed yet! The Bible does not possess magical power on its own. Reading it without God's Spirit will simply make you a Pharisee.

The only acceptable way to approach the Bible is with a hunger to know God Himself.

If this is a new perspective for you, consider this analogy. Imagine a man sent a love letter to his girlfriend. She was so excited to receive it that she read it over and over again, memorizing every part of it, learning to quote it, and studying the word choice. She learned everything she could know about him from the letters— what he liked and didn't like, what he had done in his past, what he expected out of her. Yet, when the man came to meet her in person, she was not interested in talking to him. She was so caught up in the letter, that the letter had *become* her boyfriend!

This sounds absurd, but it is exactly how many Christians treat the Bible. They love the Bible more than being with God. But the Bible was given to us to help us know and recognize God! It grieves His heart when we turn His love letter into an idol. Then what He gave to show the way of life becomes a way of death.

What this means is that in order to really understand God's Word, you must invite Him into the process. You must focus on Him. If in your heart you want to know the Bible for its own sake, then you have to repent before it is of any value to you. In fact, I suggest not reading it at all for awhile until you are more interested in knowing God than doing your quiet time.

The Christian life is not about performance—do you want the living God or not? Only when your heart begins to crave a relationship with God will you be able to hear what He is saying to you in His letter. It will ring with truth because you know Him.

THE FINAL AUTHORITY

Reading the Bible in a right posture along with the Holy Spirit is the best way to getting a proper interpretation because God Himself is the best interpreter of His own Word. When you are seeking a relationship with Him, and you invite Him to come illuminate his Word to you, the Holy Spirit will be there with you to make difficult things clear. He is your guide through the complicated maze of the Scripture.

This means if you add other sources of authority, those sources of authority will slowly become substitutes for the authority of God and His Word. The Bible was meant to be a complete package where God gives you what you need to know, and the Holy Spirit helps you to discover it. Enhancements were never meant to be part of the package, or they would have come with it!

Of course, tools are helpful for deep study. You can get help from friends, commentaries, or books, but when you begin to rely on something else as the key to understanding the Bible, it becomes the real Bible. You reversed the order of authority. There are streams of Christianity which encourage this worldview, sometimes inadvertently. Instead of the Bible having authority over people, churches, and all other thought, now those things have authority over the Bible. Whatever you use as a special interpretive key is now the real and final authority.

So what about deeper study? A diligent student will have teachers, study guides, and other items which help draw more insight from the Bible. But a proper resource should make the Bible's *own* message plainer. It should help unlock the Bible so you can depend on the *Bible* more—not make you more dependent on the resource. The Bible remains the filter through which other resources should pass, not vice versa. A simple test is: when the interpretive key is removed, does the Bible still clearly teach what was suggested in the key?

A "key" can be any source of authority, not just a commentary. Satan is interested in using any means available to replace God's authority with His own—even a good teacher! If he cannot physically keep the Bible from you, he may try to lock you into a system where you do not feel confident in interpreting the Bible yourself. You start to rely on others to get meaning for you. This strategy, of creating another authority other than God's Word and

Spirit, can have a variety of faces. Here are some of the most common ones:

- **The Church**: The Catholic emphasis on the Church having the only correct interpretation of Scripture leads Church doctrine to replace the Bible. Authority is in the Church rather than the text. This can happen in other denominations too. When what you believe is simply what your church or denomination says, you have exchanged the traditions of men for the Word of God.

- **A Person**: Emphasizing that a reading must be true because it came from your pastor or favorite teacher, is another way of supplanting the authority of God's Word. In fact, this is how cults are formed. Just because a leader is charismatic or has a powerful anointing does not mean his or her reading is correct.

- **Bible + Special Text.** Many cults base themselves on the Bible, but an additional text is always required to get the correct interpretation. The Mormons have the Book of Mormon. The Jehovah's Witnesses have the Watchtower. Christians can also fall into this trap when certain books or guides are elevated as the key to correct theology. A manmade text now has authority to shape or correct the Bible.

- **Allegorical Keys.** When someone has interpreted certain parts of the Bible to represent other things, this leads you to rely on their allegory to understand the Bible. This can be seen, for example, in some Christians' reliance on dispensational charts to understand the book of Revelation. A manmade construct now has authority.

There are other, more subtle ways the authority of the Holy Spirit can be traded for man's, under the guise of being academic:

- **Original Language Expertise**: Emphasizing that you must know Greek/Hebrew to understand the Bible is very common. This places interpretation in the hands of specialists, who can hide their interpretation in the meanings of words.

- **Background Information:** Some teach that the real meaning of a passage can only be determined when you fully understand the ancient world in which it was spoken. This leads you to do vast investigation and research in extra-Biblical texts to determine the meaning of a passage.

- **Higher Criticism.** Higher Critics are Bible skeptics who say only parts of the Bible are true. This shifts the real authority to the interpreter who chooses which parts are divine and reliable for you, and which are not.

- **Source Criticism.** Source critics focus on finding new, various authors of Biblical books—some other, unknown author wrote the source document for Matthew and Mark, for example. This makes you think the Bible really should read some other way. These hidden texts have the authority instead of the Bible we all have. Or the critics do, as the experts.

The common thread between all of these is moving the interpretation of the Bible away from the average reader and into the hands of an elite few. Each false authority has the "real" meaning of the text which can only be known if you know or do something extra, not contained in the Bible itself. Not only does this remove your motivation to study the Bible, it makes the church vulnerable to false interpretations. Don't fall for these traps! While some resources do aid in understanding the text, none are necessary to grow into relationship with God. Only the Holy Spirit and a pure heart are. Recognize these reasons as Satanic in origin, trying to make you doubt God's Word is enough.

FAITH, LOVE, AND THE HERMENEUTICAL SPIRAL

We explained at the beginning of the chapter that the first and most important part of interpreting the Bible is what is in your heart while you are reading. Every person brings a set of hidden assumptions about themselves and God to their reading. When you bring false notions about God to the Scripture, you get false readings. But when you bring correct notions about God to the Scripture, it opens up even more.

How do we know that? Because the Bible says so. By reading the Bible, you learn how to read the Bible. This sounds like circular reasoning doesn't it? Theologians have a term for this – the *hermeneutical spiral*. You study various parts of the Bible, and from these parts you develop principles. Then you take those principles and apply them back to the text so you can understand it even more. This leads you to develop new or deeper principles, and the process starts all over again.

This can continue for an entire lifetime. The principles you develop are really your theology which you then bring back into the text when you interpret it. When you find something in the text that does not fit your theology, you may need to change or refine it, and start the process over again.

This sounds confusing, but it is just a form of the scientific method applied to the Bible. It is a way of developing a theory from doing an experiment and then seeing if your theory is correct by applying it to more experiments.

You can see how it works with the principle, for example, that God is love. This is one of the most important principles the Bible teaches, and is required to interpret the Bible correctly. First it is taught explicitly: "God is love, and the one who remains in love remains in God, and God remains in him," (1 John 4:16). So you understand that love is not just an attribute of God; it is a defining element of His character.

Then you apply it back to what you're reading. You see the epistles as love, the gospel as love, even the entire Bible as love—a story of God reaching out to be reconciled with humanity, culminating with sending Jesus as the ultimate act of love. Love is now your interpretive principle. It will lead you to different interpretations than before—and more accurate theology—because only when you have a deep abiding belief that God is always acting from a heart of profound love, can you properly understand what He is doing throughout the Bible.

This is the hermeneutical spiral in operation. There are many difficult passages in the Bible which may cause you to question the love of God. But questioning His love will not lead you to correct Bible interpretation. In fact, it closes the text to you. If you fear God is not really loving, you will end up confirming that fear from the text. You may fall into works or away from God completely because the heart can't stay soft towards a God who isn't loving.

Instead, you must work backwards in faith, to the passage which is challenging you. God plainly states throughout the Scripture that He is infinitely loving, so you must evaluate the text you are reading through this lens.

As another example, take Jesus' rebuke of the Pharisees in the book of Matthew. It goes on for several chapters and is quite severe. It is easy in our human minds to see Jesus as simply angry. Yet, a deeper understanding allows you to see that this was in fact the best way to love the hardened Pharisees, as well as love those whom their religious system was oppressing. Condemnation was what the Pharisees needed to hear in order to give them the possibility of repenting, and it was what common people needed to hear in order to have faith to abandon the oppressive system they kept being told was correct.

Similar applications can be made throughout the Old Testament when you presuppose God's loving character. True Bible study works in this way, moving you away from shallow interpretations. This is reading in faith, and the Holy Spirit will keep opening your eyes to deeper revelation on it.

A second important principle is the principle of faith: God always requires faith to have a relationship. The more faith, the more relationship; the less faith, the less relationship.

In Genesis, for example, Cain approaches God with the fruit of his human effort. Abel approaches God knowing that human effort will not be acceptable, relying on a sacrifice to make him right. Cain receives correction and Abel receives a blessing. The person who is trying to approach God by works will see an endless list of rules and a corrective God who unfairly condemns. But Paul says, "the Law has become our tutor to lead us to Christ, so that we may be justified by faith." The more you try to live by the Law and relate to God on the basis of human effort, the more hopeless you will feel. This was done on purpose to make you realize you need a Savior to stand in your place. As long as you still live in fear of the Law, trying to be as good as you can, you're not accepting you need a Savior. You're still offering Cain's gift instead of Abel's.

Faith affects Bible interpretation. Many think the Bible is a hopeless string of fear-inspiring condemnations, but this is seeing things through the eyes of Cain. Through the eyes of Abel, you have a new lens for reading the Bible. Through faith in the sacrifice of Jesus, you see He is not burdening you or people in the Bible with heavy lists, but is instead exhorting everyone to return to Him.

In the Old Testament books of the prophets, for example, although there are many charges that God could pick to level against Israel, His primary focus is always that the people have gone after idols. The kings who tear down the idols are considered righteous not because they strictly observe the Law, but because they turned their hearts to God. God wants this and blesses those who keep seeking Him and trusting Him, like David, even though by the Law they are far from perfect.

The same principle applies to Jesus' teaching in the Sermon on the Mount (Matthew 5-7). These impossible commands are designed to cause you to recognize your need for a Savior. No one can possibly perfectly obey them—they are in fact the highest standard of the Law. But when you approach God through faith in Jesus, relying on His righteousness, not your own, you can receive the favor and love of God. You even have grace to approximate those principles. The commandments become encouragements because you know He is not condemning you over them but is pointing out what is true and possible when people follow Him.

The point is that reading the Bible helps you to read the Bible, but you have to read in faith and love. The Bible instructs you to do that, and when you do, it opens up. All of a sudden you find yourself in relationship with God, having a deeper experience with Him because you believe the right things.

But believing these things takes some willingness to repent and change. This is how the hermeneutical spiral works— being willing to see causes more to be seen. Jesus explains this when the people ask Him why He speaks in parables, rather than just straight out. Jesus explains that the element of faith is necessary to know the truth:

> *"The knowledge of the secrets of the kingdom of heaven has been given to you, but not them [the Pharisees]. Whoever has will be given more, and they will have an abundance. Whoever does not have, even what they have will be taken away from them. This is why I speak in parables...But blessed are your eyes because they see and your ears because they hear." (Matthew 13:11-16).*

This is your assurance—that if your heart is right and you put some effort into having the correct interpretive principles, God will be with you and reveal whatever you need to know.

Chapter 13:
God's Symbolic Language

God's Word is spoken very simply. Much of it is through stories and parables. In the educated Western world, we have been separated from story-based learning through technology and secondary education. From the legacy of the ancient Greeks, we have learned to think in terms of principles and abstractions rather than objects.

This can make it difficult for us to directly understand and receive a revelation that, to others, might be more obvious. Those who possess less education, both in the Western world and all over the developing world, do not think in terms of abstractions—they think in terms of the real and concrete. The stories and images of the Bible may connect with them more because they think in the terms that God spoke the Bible in.

In the West, we must, in some sense, relearn how to think in imagery and stories if we want to understand God's Word fully. Sometimes we forget that God created the world and everything in it. Every plant, every physical process, every animal—they were all created by God, and they are all an expression of His identity. When God refers to them, in some sense He is speaking His own native language – the one He created when He made the universe.

When God uses a symbol in the Bible, therefore, it is not simply that He is making an analogy to something external. He is revealing something about Himself and the way He created the world.

Take the seed, for example. When God created the world, he placed man in a fruit-bearing garden and commanded him to cultivate it. The prophets, wisdom books, and Jesus' teaching help us to understand the many aspects of God's character and universe which are revealed in the simple seed. First there is the principle of reaping and sowing, and how you get more of what you planted. Secondly, there is the idea that something has its full nature when it is in seed form—it simply must grow. Third, is the idea that a seed must be nurtured. Then there is the idea that something must die in order for the seed to be planted and grow. Just the single idea of a seed is so rich, you could write a whole book developing it, which touches on the brilliance of God.

The point is that God isn't accidentally using the seed to speak to us. The seed which He created encapsulates something about how He works, and how the universe He created is designed. Furthermore, He knows mankind has been acquainted with seeds since the dawn of time. The process of planting and cultivating are almost universal, and lead to understanding some of the most basic aspects of God's nature.

Therefore, it is important to understand that unlike other works of literature where symbols can be rooted in any idea, Biblical symbols are rooted in creation. You can understand God's language once you meditate on how He created the world. In that sense, the Bible is an extended commentary on the creation. The Old Testament illuminates the creation, the New Testament illuminates the Old Testament, and the outworking of the gospel in the church age illuminates the New Testament. Each one builds and expands on what was revealed before.

WHAT A TYPE REALLY IS

When God created the world, He brought His eternal identity into material form. Something like the seed therefore represents an aspect of God's character which is true in any context and at any scale. Consider the fact that a seed is the entire identity of the plant, in a tiny unit. As that seed grows, it becomes a plant, and as that plant grows, it can become an entire forest. The identity of the seed has not changed, only the scale and context of the seed has changed.

This is the way symbols work in the Bible. The context may change, the scale may change, but the fundamental identity of a specific symbol does not change. The type can be woven through the entire Bible, starting with the creation itself.

Consider robes or garments. In the beginning, Adam and Eve were naked and needed no clothing. However, when they sinned, they realized they needed a covering so they made a garment. The first garment came into existence because of sin. This is its "created" identity hinted at in Genesis. What happened next was that they had to remove their manmade garments in order to accept a better garment from God. God replaced their manmade method of dealing with sin with His own method of dealing with sin. God took them out from under their own authority and put them under His covering or authority.

Therefore, the garment has both a dark and a light side – a garment made by man to cover you is bad, but a garment made by God to cover you is good. Depending on the context, it can represent either how sin is dealt with, how authority is passed, or both.

This is not simply a little story from Genesis. The garment is a *type*, which means an idea reappearing and developing throughout the Bible. We see the garment again in the story of Joseph where he is given an amazing robe—a sign of God's brilliant covering or authority. The robe is then passed back to Jacob in darkness and deception, as a manmade cover to the brothers' sin.

Later, Elijah casts his garment or mantle onto Elisha as a sign of passing his God-given authority on. After that, Jesus has His robe stripped from Him and divided up among the people. And finally in Revelation, Jesus promises to give those who overcome a spotless robe. The fundamental function of the garment never changes each time it appears, but the context changes. It grows in meaning from Genesis to Revelation.

Understanding that the essence or function of something matters, not its scale or context, helps you understand the Bible as a whole.

For example, the Bible refers to nations in terms of who their ancestors were. "Esau" can refer to either the individual Esau, or it can refer to the people descended from Esau – the Edomites. "Moab" was an entire people group, but it was also the name of Lot's son who founded the city of Moab. The term is used interchangeably to refer to either individual or descendants, because from a Biblical perspective, the essence of the nation and the man were the same. One simply developed from the other.

As you understand the function of a symbol in its context, you are able to explore the deeper meaning implied by the story. You can do this both forwards and backwards. As you learn about a symbol in one place, you can apply that understanding to another.

Types are continuous threads which run through the Bible. When a symbol, name, or even phrase reappears, it hearkens back to what was said about it before. And it foreshadows what will be said about it again. Understanding this interrelated system helps you develop the meaning which might be easily missed by the naked eye.

Typology, or the study of types, can even help outside of Biblical interpretation. In recent years, a great deal has been written and taught on dream interpretation as the Church has begun to officially recognize that God still speaks through dreams and visions. Dreams are almost always highly symbolic events where God communicates important ideas to you through symbols.

Our standard approach to Scripture makes this seem a very difficult and foreign process, but when you switch to an approach to Scripture which incorporates symbolic meaning like typology, you will naturally develop many of the faculties needed to interpret dreams properly. In fact, all the major dreams listed in the Bible – those given to Pharaoh and the rulers of Babylon—can be easily interpreted once you understand the role of symbols in God's communicative vocabulary.

LITERARY DEVICES

God's thematic continuity is not simply limited to physical objects. It is also seen in the use of language in the Bible. When a phrase reappears in the Bible, it is a way of intentionally importing the meaning of a previous text.

For example, Adam was told to "guard and keep" the Garden of Eden. Later in the Law, the priests are told to "guard and keep" the temple using the exact same Hebrew phrase. By using that same phrase, the Bible intentionally connects the function Adam had in the garden with the function the priests had in the temple. This kind of reference then sheds light on both. We see Adam was doing a kind of priestly function and the priesthood was doing a kind of Adamic function. Just like a priest, Adam was God's representative on earth, assigned to guard His presence and mediate it on earth.

Also the priesthood, by leavening the territory of Israel, was an extension of what Adam was assigned to do in the Garden. This connection can be further developed by exploring all of the various functions of the priest, even their garments and equipment, and how it illuminates the function of Adam in the Garden, who himself was the priest for all mankind.

Now just like in literature, some connections are stronger and some are weaker. Some are clearly intended by the text, some are just hinted at, and some are a matter of speculation. You can't form a doctrine out of something speculative, but you can profitably explore it. You can use it for your own personal application and to develop and support more clearly intended doctrines.

Comparison and contrast is another major literary device used by the Biblical authors to bring forth meaning. Take, for example, Proverbs 12:4:

> *A wife of noble character is her husband's crown,*
> *But a disgraceful wife is like decay in his bones.*

Like many of the proverbs, this stanza is written in a **parallelism**. In a parallelism, the lines either repeat the same themes using different words, or contrasts a theme with its opposite. These structures can be built up in very complex ways, but the way that they work is to bring forth richer meaning through comparison.

In this example, we have two very straightforward statements which could stand all on their own. However, when you start to contrast them, you find more substance. A wife of noble character is being contrasted here with a disgraceful wife. This means that one of the attributes of a wife of noble character is causing the opposite of disgrace—she causes her husband to be exalted. The husband's "crown" is set in parallel with "decay in his bones." This is implying that being exalted is the opposite of having decay in your bones, and therefore one of the aspects of being exalted is being free from this undermining effect.

In a **contrasting parallelism**, you learn more about how two things differ, whereas in a **comparison parallelism**, the original theme is reinforced or developed further. For example, in Psalm 15:1 there is a comparison:

> Who may dwell in your sanctuary?
> Who may live on your holy hill?

In this parallelism, the same thing is being said twice. This allows us to associate the idea of God's sanctuary with His holy hill. The Bible is implying there is something the same or similar about them. In what ways are the sanctuary and the holy hill the same? In what ways are they different?

First, take it beyond this immediate text. What Biblical ideas does a "holy hill" bring up for you? God encountered Abraham on a mountain, met with Moses on the mountain, and also met with Jesus on a mountain. As you begin to reflect on it, you might observe that these encounters were a kind of sanctuary. Remember how Jesus went to the mountain with Peter, James, and John before His final days of ministry, and how they wanted to stay there? What things happened on that mountain that made it a sanctuary? God's presence was there. God's presence to you is a kind of sanctuary, a "holy hill" in which you can take refuge.

These are a very simple parallelisms on a very small scale, but larger and much more complex parallelisms exist throughout the Bible. Judah and Joseph are two characters presented as parallel stories. Many of the same themes appear, they are just inverted. Joseph is tempted by a woman, but he responds rightly. Judah is tempted by a woman, but he falls. Both stories involve a deception involving a garment and a goat. In the first story the deception succeeds, and in the second it fails. Both stories involve the death of a son, in the first he is mourned, and in the second he is hardly remembered.

These are only just a few of the parallels! They are easily overlooked, but once you find them it is unmistakable that the story was told in the Bible in such a way to highlight the contrast in character between the two men. Each aspect that you examine, can unfold revelation. How were the two men different, and how were they the same? By comparing and contrasting the two of them, you gain more insight than if you read about one of them alone.

When we discover these kinds of literary links in larger narratives, something larger about the way the Bible was written comes into focus: the Author is intentionally telling the story to make it connect with the larger narrative. The images He chooses to use are hooks which connect a story to the stories around it, and the entire story of the Bible.

For instance, if God had told the story of Judah without any interest in the larger narrative, it is unlikely He would have highlighted features like the goat and the garment – since it's really a story about inheritance. God does this to force a real event to connect with the larger typological story. This could be called the **forced parallelism** of the Bible. Biblical authors retell events in ways that force them to elaborate eternal themes.

This isn't just the way the Old Testament was written. The gospels are written this way too. According to John, Jesus did so many things that it would have been impossible to even retell them all (John 21:25). So he and the other gospel writers had to select their material. They did so in very specific ways.

As more study has gone into these books, this becomes increasingly clear. Matthew is not just a collection of stories—it is organized to present Jesus as the founder of a new Israel, and demonstrate all the ways Jesus repeated and fulfilled the entire history of Israel. For instance, it tells about how Jesus was taken into Egypt like Joseph, but came out like Moses. And how He had to meet Satan in the wilderness just like Joseph, Moses, and the Israelites did. Jesus went to a mountain and gave a new Law like Moses. He entered the Promised Land after being baptized in the Jordan like Joshua, and then finally emerged as King of Jerusalem like David.

This isn't just what happened, it is how the story is told. Matthew intentionally connects and creates parallels between real events through the use of images, which expand on the themes God cares about.

This is the way the Bible fundamentally communicates. It is not separated into tiny little pieces that have no relationship. It is exactly the opposite. Every piece contains something that can shine light on another piece. What you learn from one reference illuminates another reference, or even the whole Bible.

Studying the Bible is the process of interweaving and decoding, understanding on more and more fundamental levels what God is saying and how He says it. Beginning to notice and explore the symbols God speaks through will help you get the fullness of Scriptural counsel on a subject. The next section includes a chart which will help you do this.

MULTIPLE APPLICATIONS

In light of the Bible's integrated nature, the notion that you should focus on a single piece of it is hard to defend. As you approach the Bible looking for answers, God can use the entire tapestry, or just a single section to speak to you. Furthermore, while a given text should certainly be thought of as having one primary historical meaning – the plain and obvious one – once you begin to see the rich and interwoven nature of the text, it becomes clear that the idea of a "single" interpretation is silly.

The Biblical text is an expression of God's eternal truth in a given place and time. A later author, preacher, or you yourself can pick up on this theme and develop it further, bringing meaning out of the text which may not have originally been in the mind of author. The interpretation must be consistent with the author's originally essential intent, but just as the prophets spoke things that they had no way of fully understanding the full meaning of, so all Biblical texts have the potential to expand beyond what was said to the original author. This is sometimes called the **sensus plenior** or "fuller meaning" of the text.

The question is how can you bridge to these fuller meanings? What are the connecting points? This brings us into the realm of application. Application is the process of making what the Bible said in the past come alive to those living now. In an application, you are not searching for the timeless doctrines which can be put on a statement of faith, but for the specific meanings relevant to your situation. You can bridge to application in several main ways: directly, symbolically, through recontexualization, and psychologically.

Direct application is the most straightforward kind. In this method, those in the Bible are held up as models, and you simply imply that you are to emulate what they did. For example, the Bible says Hezekiah lived by faith; therefore you should also live by faith.

Symbolic interpretation builds on typology. Any aspect of a story can be symbolic or treated as symbolic as long as it is consistent with the overall use of symbols in the Bible and in creation. The famous story of Elisha causing the axe head to float invites many different symbolic interpretations. An axe is something sharp, so it could represent the "edge" or cutting power of the prophetic ministry at that time. An axe head also is an instrument of human effort, so it could represent what can be accomplished in human strength. The axe head is also something heavy, so it could be compared to something heavy.

You can't make authoritative doctrine out of any of these interpretations, but you can build a fascinating example of a larger Biblical point. Symbolic application therefore brings forth meaning by giving some aspect of the story a much larger meaning than is explained on the surface. An attribute of an object, person, relationship, or place can be broadened to represent something beyond its immediate context.

Recontextualization is a technique of recasting what the Bible said into modern terms and situations to make it more understandable to the hearer. By comparing an ancient king with the President of the United States, or the Jewish temple with the U.S. Capitol, you can make the gap between the message and the hearer much smaller, therefore helping them understand how their experience is fundamentally the same as Biblical experience.

This can also be done by contrast. By drawing out how what happened in the Bible was fundamentally different than what is happening now, you can help bridge to application.

Psychological assumption is a method of expanding on what is plainly stated in the text. One of the things you must understand when reading the Bible is that it understates and hints at many things, rather than fully developing them.

Perhaps this was for brevity or to leave room for the interpreter. But whatever the reason, much is left to the imagination. The Bible invites you to interrogate it: Why did this happen this way? Could it have happened another way? Why did people react the way they did? What do the circumstances imply the characters were feeling? There are many "blanks" to fill in. Psychological assumption fills them in.

As an example, consider the story of Jacob. We are not told a lot about Jacob's feelings, but if you understand human nature, it is not hard to guess what they were, or to get a sense of the kind of man he was. He deceived his brother and ran away from home. What kinds of emotions would he have been experiencing in this situation? The Bible does not tell us, but human experience does. Similarly, you can imagine his anger and disappointment on the morning he woke up and discovered he had been given the wrong wife!

Our understanding of human nature allows us to enrich and further interpret what is only hinted at in the text. This kind of assumption can be done based on human nature, the character's record, or the story up to that point. It can be based on contextual clues or even pure speculation. All of these allow you to move to an application of the text.

This method can be seen in the way that Peter interprets Lot's flight from Sodom.

> *He rescued righteous Lot, greatly distressed by the sensual conduct of the wicked, for as that righteous man lived among them day after day, he was tormenting his righteous soul over their lawless deeds that he saw and heard. (2 Peter 2:7-8)*

There is nothing in the original Genesis account to indicate Lot's psychological state while living in Sodom. We are only given the bare facts of the case including that Lot was a righteous man whom God wanted to save and that he responded graciously when the angels showed up. We know, in contrast, that the city was very wicked and attacked Lot because they wanted to abuse the angels.

From these facts, it is natural to assume that a righteous man living in such a wicked place would have been vexed, but it is not explicitly stated in the text. There is no way Peter could have known anything about something which had occurred some 2000 years earlier except that, under the leading of the Holy Spirit, he made a psychological assumption which was consistent with what was known about Lot and human nature.

Some have even gone a step farther to argue that the Biblical text is intentionally written to facilitate this kind of interpretation. If you are a careful reader of the Scripture you may have noticed how often information which would psychologically connect things together are missing.

On the one hand, this could be considered a form of dramatic understatement, or a stylistic nuance of ancient writing. But it could also be considered an *interpretive gap* which was part of God's design. The fact that such details are almost always omitted from the story invites the reader to engage in speculation, which is a reflective process that teaches us about our own hearts and about the human condition. The process of filling in the interpretive gap is what draws you personally into the story.

These are only a few of the ways that the Holy Spirit can bring fuller meaning out of a passage. The Holy Spirit is extremely creative. What He can do with a particular text and how He can connect it to real life are often quite amazing.

EXAMINING A THEME

Since the Bible has thematic development and continuity throughout, it can be extremely enriching to look at a theme, image, or even a phrase or word as it develops in the Bible. The approach we have been advocating is to take into account the entire Bible in order to properly interpret the text.

We have included a chart at the end of this chapter to help you do this. It is not a "method," but simply a tool which can help you start to think in terms of the whole Bible instead of just isolated parts.

As you learned earlier, the Bible has sections which are very distinct from one another. They are different in in terms of how far along they are in the story, and they are different in terms of the way language is used. Some books, like Revelation, are highly symbolic and others, like Paul's epistles, are much more literal. Regardless, every major theme and almost all minor themes will show up in every section of the Bible in some way or another.

In order to use the chart, start with any passage, idea, or concept you want to examine and write it in the chart. Then search for at least one major related item in a different section of the Bible. What you are looking for may change depending on where you are in the Bible.

For example, if you wanted to examine the doctrine of hell, traditionally you might try to gather all the verses where hell is explicitly referenced and fuse them together into a theology. This will lead to some good insights but may omit some things. For instance, Jesus talks about hell, and Revelation shows us a picture of hell, but what about Genesis? When Jesus referred to the final judgment, He referenced the story of Sodom and Gomorrah, so Sodom and Gomorrah is a "seed" of what eventually develops into the doctrine of hell.

What about the Law? There is the story of Korah's rebellion where the earth opens up and swallows Korah. What about the wisdom books? In Job, "the deep" or "abyss" is discussed. Go through the Bible and find all the connections you can, even if they are loose.

Then, apply what you learn from one place to each of the other Scriptures. That's what the last line in the box is for. For example, if Sodom is a type of hell, what can we learn about hell and who goes there? It was a judgment of literal fire and sulfur which suggests that hell will be a place of literal fire, even though Paul does not explicitly say this. Also, hellfire broke out when all the righteous had been completely removed. Does this connect to what will happen at the last judgment? Or, if Sodom is a type of hell, is Sodom referenced anywhere else? What can we learn from those references?

Good interpretation is like pulling on a thread. You follow it wherever it leads, back and forth through the Bible, until you have completely exhausted the concept. Remember, the Bible story is a trajectory. Everything important starts in creation or Genesis, and builds throughout the Bible until Revelation. It may only be hinted at in the beginning and then developed as a major theme later on.

For instance, there is only a hint of a temple in the Garden of Eden, but there are many chapters on it in the Law. Then in Revelation, heaven itself is alluded to as a temple. So you are not just looking at cross-references, you are looking at a progressive development of a theme.

If you are examining an object like "fire" or "garment," then the chart included at the end of this chapter has a box for the function of that object in creation. For example, fire burns, purifies, and destroys. Therefore, images associated with fire throughout the Bible are going to be somehow connected to these functions. As you read through the various passages where fire is referenced, this background may enrich your understanding.

CONCLUSION

The study of Biblical interpretation is a complicated and vast problem domain. This section has tried to resolve just some of the issues associated with interpretation, and start you down a path to understanding the fullness of Scripture.

We have tried to avoid rehashing material which is widely and easily available through standard texts. We have also critiqued the most commonly taught method of Bible interpretation in seminaries. This is in part because we believe that background study and original language study should be only a small part of the interpretive process, not the dominant feature that they are now.

Instead, we have focused on how to help you move into a Spirit-filled method of interpretation that is still fully Word-based. What the Church needs to sustain revived Christians is this kind of a method which focuses on life and depth of relationship with God. We hope we have started you down that path.

	Creation	Genesis	Law	History	Wisdom Prophets	Gospels Acts	Epistles	Revelation
	Creation Function	Seeds	Principles	Examples	Alluded to	How Fulfilled	How Applied	Spiritual Realities
Scripture References								
Meaning in Context								
Apply insights from other contexts to this context								

Appendix: KJV Only?

KING JAMES ONLY?

In the last century, as modern Bible translations have taken off and popular Bible speakers each have their own version of the Bible that they love, many faithful believers have been concerned about the modernization and corruption of the original Scriptures. Some have embraced the traditional view that the King James is the only reliable version of the Bible. This movement has waned in influence over the last decade or so, but is still popular and of great important in some circles.

For centuries, English speakers had only one major choice—the King James Bible. There had been previous English Bibles such as the Tyndale Bible and the Great Bible, but King James I of England attempted to standardize the Bible in by subsidizing his own official version for all.

The KJV was known officially as the Authorized Version (AV), and became, for many people, *the* Bible. Some have made the argument that the King James Bible is the only acceptable translation. Purists will even insist that it be the 1611 edition, not a later one.

But it's important to remember all the major battles that were fought through history to bring the Bible to the language of the *common man* – first Greek, then Latin, then common English, and now into thousands of common languages all across the world. Remember the Protestant Reformers' fight was to get the Bible in language that people could understand, as easily as anything else they read. Many Reformers even died for this cause.

Catching the spirit of this is key to the right perspective of the KJV. Can you imagine Martin Luther being upset if you told him his German Bible from the 1500s had to be replaced with a more modern one, so more Germans today could understand it? Wasn't that his point in the first place?

Similarly, four hundred years later, King James English is not the language of the common English-speaking person anymore—it is the language of Shakespeare. Many words have changed in meaning and connotation such as *"Suffer* the little children…" This can lead readers to draw inaccurate conclusions.

Other words are completely obsolete—do you know what "betimes," "blain," or "bruit" mean? King James English is beautiful, but except for those who were raised on it, increasingly challenging to read and understand properly. It can even be a stumbling block to those hearing the gospel and trying to grow in it.

Another way to look at the issue is, do we currently translate the Bible into missionary languages based on how they used to be spoken in the past, or how they are spoken now? If we do not have a problem translating the Bible into other languages for other people groups, we should not have a problem translating the Bible into modern English for ourselves.

Respectfully, the "Authorized Version" was authorized by King James I, not by God. King James didn't even authorize it for the godliest reasons. He authorized it because the Bible that the English Reformers used, the Geneva Bible, had notes in the margins that were hostile to his kingship, Catholicism, and the Anglican church… all things he cared about. During its translation, the King James editors ended up relying on the Geneva Bible anyway, but King James deleted the notes in the margin and ensured the Bible supported his own authority. This caused believers like William Bradford and the Pilgrims to reject it; they didn't want their Scripture authorized by a king who was persecuting them. They brought the Geneva Bible to the early American colonies instead.

The fact that the KJV is so widely used today is less a sign of a special stamp of approval by God, and more of a sign of the great success of the British Empire over the centuries.

But isn't the King James is the most "pure" translation, compared to the others? The fact is, that no English translation can live up to this claim because the Bible was originally written in Hebrew and Greek. Translation from one language to another always involves some degree of choice and interpretation by the translator.

Additionally, a Biblical text is always limited by the best ancient manuscripts you have at the time. Later on, better ones will be discovered which will force you to revise your older translations. The KJV was not beyond these limitations and its translators acknowledged that. In their preface, they wrote that "imperfections and blemishes may be noted," and that the text should stay "current." Their work was the best they could do at the time, but they knew it would require an update eventually.

Only two years later, they did so. A second KJV edition was released in 1613 with corrections. Today we know the ancient manuscripts they had to rely on were not the oldest and best available. It is sometimes said that the KJV authors used the "*textus receptus*" or "received text," which makes some people feel the text is a divine miracle, "received" from heaven. But the translators actually used the Stephanus 3rd edition of the Greek New Testament as their source document. That name is pretty normal sounding, isn't it?

And while the Greek New Testament was much better than the Latin, it was still several centuries before all the Greek, Coptic, Syriac, and other manuscripts were found and could be examined for accuracy. What was eventually discovered was that similar kinds of things which had been added to the Latin text had also crept into the Greek text over time. When very old manuscripts were found, like the *Codex Sinaiticus* which was a direct copy dating to around 330AD, this became clear. Contemporary Bible versions sometimes note that the editors have "deleted" some verses. This is because they aren't in the oldest manuscripts to date.

There was a time when unbelieving scholars used these kinds of findings to try to invalidate the Bible, but as time went on, more educated believers got involved in the process. One of them, Bruce Metzger, was not just involved but became one of the most important figures in 20th century textual criticism.

In fact, every major translation of the Bible used by evangelicals today has been translated exclusively by Bible believers. Those who translated the NIV, NASB, ESV, and others all believed the gospel, knew Greek and Hebrew well, and did their best to bring the Bible into modern English. In other words, they were doing exactly what the KJV translators did hundreds of years ago.

In conclusion, if you really want a pure text, you have to do what every translator has ever done: read the Scripture in ancient Hebrew and Greek, in the most ancient manuscripts you have, then make the best decisions you can. Since we can't all do that, there is some faith involved in the process.

All of us have a desire to have the best possible version of the Bible in our hands, but sometimes our desire to have *the* Word of God can get ahead of us. You can start exalting the text itself to the point where it seems like the *Bible* is God, instead of God Himself. God inspired the originals, but they have come to us through a long and complex process.

CONCLUSION

The best Bible translation is the one that happens between your head and your heart. Don't get so hung up on mechanics or academics that you miss the point of having the Bible, which is to encounter the living God. The most important thing you need when studying the Bible is the presence of God.

No translation or format can substitute for that. It is more important to meditate on the Scripture and let it change you, than it is to accumulate large amounts of time buried in the text.

So, find a Bible you enjoy reading, and dig into it! Meditate on it, and act on it. One popular stream of worship encourages people to say it, pray it, sing it, do it. Ask the Holy Spirit to show you the truth and make its meaning clear to you. He will then help you apply it in a real, living way...which is why God wrote it in the first place.

Made in the USA
Monee, IL
01 September 2019